CONNECTICUT LITERARY ANTHOLOGY

Fiction, Poetry, and Nonfiction from the Nutmeg State

2023

2023 CONNECTICUT LITERARY ANTHOLOGY

Victoria Buitron

woodhall press

Woodhall Press | Norwalk, CT

woodhall press

Woodhall Press, Norwalk, CT 06855
WoodhallPress.com

Cover design: Danny Meoño
Layout artist: L.J. Mucci

Library of Congress Cataloging-in-Publication Data available

ISBN 978-1-954907-94-2 (paper: alk paper)
ISBN 978-1-954907-95-9 (electronic)

First Edition
Distributed by Independent Publishers Group
(800) 888-4741

Printed in the United States of America

Table of Contents

Foreword

In the process of compiling the nonfiction, fiction, and poetry that appears in this third anthology of its kind, I learned that the origins of the word Connecticut are often attributed to the language of the Algonquians—one of the ancestral residents of this land. According to the U.S. Department of Interior Indian Affairs, the original word—Quonoktacut—can be defined as "long river." And the landscape of a river is precisely how I envision the form of this anthology: a flow of vivid memories, hawks, and thistles flying underneath a dwindling sun, foxes hiding behind the flora of lush woods, and fierce currents teeming with life. The 2023 Connecticut Literary Anthology is powerful, enduring, and a necessary body of work from established and emerging writers who live throughout the state.

The book contains work from Nutmeg writers by way of Croatia, Panama, Dominican Republic, Puerto Rico, and more. Like many of the featured writers, I was not born in Connecticut, but I have made my life in it. The state belongs to me—just like it does to every writer whose work appears in this anthology. Regardless of the stated premises or settings, each piece was written by someone molded by the mere fact of being a Connecticut resident. Their work is imbued by diverse lived experiences and whatever has brought them to currently call this state their home.

I vehemently believe that literature should not just be written, but heard. It is a privilege that these writers can come together in Hartford for the Connecticut Literary Festival to read their spectacular work out loud. Beyond this biannual festival, these contributors attend readings at local libraries, form literary panels within and outside of the state, and participate in local open mics around the counties that make up Connecticut. For example, back in December 2022, I accepted a poem for publication in this anthology, and a few days later I attended an open mic at a local meet-up in Norwalk, CT. One of the attendees stood on the stage—and with neither of us knowing the other was present—read one of the poems that appears in this anthology. Listening to work read aloud by its creator gives more meaning to the work—hearing the vowels they decide to linger on, the speed of their words, and their gaze toward the audience. After reading this collection, I invite you to attend a local literary event. Yes, read Connecticut authors, but most of all—celebrate them in person with thunderous applause.

Woodhall Press expresses its gratitude to each of the writers who submitted work to the anthology. I'd like to specially thank Christopher Madden and Gates MacPherson for their support and guidance throughout this process. It was a joy to read all the submitted work, and it brought me equal joy to compile these following 46 pieces of work. I hope you enjoy them, and that they beckon you—from time to time—to revisit this river of Connecticut literature.

Victoria Buitron

Nonfiction

Staghorn Sumac and Tree of Heaven

By Sonya Huber

Each day on my commute to work on I-95 in Connecticut, my tires crossed an invisible scar marking one of the sites of greatest inequality in the United States: the line between the town of Fairfield and the city of Bridgeport. In my metal and glass carapace I mulled over the line's meaning. Each day it was a flicker, there and gone. What I wanted was to slow that interaction down, to dig into it in its presence and past. I wanted to reject the illusion of the highway, which implies progress along a number line, which tells us the answer is always ahead and that we can exit wherever we'd like. The highway promised options it did not deliver, advertised mobility that it itself destroyed, and claimed an invisible neutrality that had instead circumscribed our vision.

Instead, I peered into this inequality and tracked it over time, trying to understand its origins and its scope, the more it fragmented into a range of numbers and percentages that confounded me. The very abstraction of those figures hid any connection to humanity or place, so I swung in the opposite direction, deciding in 2014 to begin walking that municipal boundary. If nothing else, my footsteps would mark what I had begun to imagine as an invisible wall.

Six years later, my piecemeal collection of boundary fragments led me back to that same highway overpass between exits 24 and 25—or rather, below it. I had been walking the messy and industrial bank of the Rooster River, which forms the lower half of this boundary, and I then lost the river in a frazzle of underbrush, small industrial sites, and luxury car lots on the former floodplain.

Peering down through the links of a fence topped with barbed wire, I saw the river glinting from a concrete basin below, flowing in through three metal tubes beneath Interstate 95. I cut behind a fenced car lot along the base of the highway's grass slope, passing a car bumper, a basketball bleached by sun, and a string of Christmas lights strewn in the weeds.

The river below, even half-ruined and polluted with *e. coli* and trace metals, worked a different magic, slowing time into an eddy of mud. Someone had left broken chunks of fancy polished stone along this side of the riverbank: veined gray-white marble and deep splotchy olive green, maybe discards from high-end countertops. Why they'd be here behind a car lot, I had no idea. I lifted a few of them, thought maybe I'd come back to take them for stepping stones in my yard, but did not.

Nearer the overpass, two lengths of thick olive-green cord had been knotted around a small tree, dangling down the jagged bank to the churned and brown river fifteen feet below. Creeping close to the edge, I brushed up against a Tree of Heaven, a plant that looks to many like the biological representation of a vacant lot. Its long stemlike branches lined with oval leaves released a smell like burnt peanut butter that would cling to my skin even after a shower.

The tree's invasiveness and willingness to grow on asphalt and in polluted soil have earned it the epithet "ghetto palm," and Betty Smith's 1943 novel *A Tree Grows in Brooklyn* captured its relentless and rapid life force: "It grows up out of cellar gratings. It is the only tree that grows out of cement. It grows lushly...survives without sun, water, and seemingly earth."

The tree had fallen down a slope from high to low status, much as the quahog hard-shell clam of this coast had been revered by the Paugussett nation and made into sacred wampum, which then became currency as trade beads for white settlers invading this coast in the 1600s, causing botanist Linnaeus to dub the quahog with the scientific name it still carries: *Mercenaria mercenaria,* literally "Money money." Taking a similar route, the Tree of Heaven as *Ailanthus altissima* was

5

brought to the U.S. in 1784 and then again in the 1820s as a status symbol by upper-class gardeners looking to add a dash of the Asian "exotic" to their gardens. Like the invasive starling—brought here as another European project to import to North America every bird mentioned in Shakespeare's plays—the Tree of Heaven spread, as white people spread, across this continent, often poisoning the soil as they went.

Tree of Heaven dispersed itself via a cunning and invisible form of botanical colonization: it killed everything around it by emitting toxic chemicals into the soil. As the tree became common, widespread, and associated with poor land and with poor people and people of color, its social meaning became a kind of biological garbage. Freed onto this landscape it grew rapidly, spreading by both root suckers and winged seed. It would not stay where it was put, it could not be controlled, and so it was discarded.

I judged this plant, this successful organism that had never asked to be here. I had never looked at it directly, but I absorbed via the lines of class and race in this country—through the land and people we discard—that this plant was "trash," and I used it somehow as a peripheral marker for places not to go, for a sign of wrongness on the landscape. Even an outlet as staid as *National Geographic* described the tree as "hellish."

As I traced its profile in guidebooks, I realized that I did and didn't know what I was seeing. I confused it, as many people do, with a native plant, Staghorn Sumac. Both have ovate leaves along long branches. As the Tree of Heaven grows rapidly skyward, Staghorn Sumac crouches with twisty, thick branches, preferring the edges of forests. In autumn the sumac offers thick reddish cones of nutritious tiny berries that impart a lemony flavor, which Indigenous people used to make a drink and Romans dried it as a spice that is still used across the Middle East.

6

What fascinated me about this area was, first, its very illegibility. Like almost all the main roads that radiated from Bridgeport, the road surrendered its identity at the border, as the river itself had been split into two names by settlers, changed from the Uncowa to the Rooster River up north and Ash Creek below. The road that once radiated from the city was named State Street, but now it crossed the river and became Commerce Avenue. State and commerce: it seemed a telling balance, stressing which side had tipped the scales.

Toward Bridgeport, a cavernous vast overpass arced skyward, casting the road into shadow. It was unlit, without sidewalks, and a truck parked idling beneath it turned it into a roaring echo chamber with pools of murky water glinting in the gloom. This was a hell-gate of sorts, promising doom to all who ventured to walk here. And no one did. From Fairfield, there was no reason to. From Bridgeport, any driver—never mind walking or riding a bike—would be suspect. Don Greenberg, a political scientist who taught at Fairfield University, described the tacit police policy of stopping drivers of color "from at least the very early 1960s to the late 1980s." Former First Selectman John Sullivan admitted in 1988 that he had approved of the practice, yet when another Fairfield University professor mentioned this fact during a campus talk on race in America, he was immediately reprimanded by both university and town and forced to publicly retract the claim.

The town of Fairfield had received a $6 million federal grant to clean up this area in 1961; the plan involved draining marshes, taking down older housing, and selling off the improved real estate in 1961. A group calling themselves Fairfielders for Property Rights took out newspaper ads in 1965 claiming that the Democratic town council intended "to bring crime, public housing, and urban renewal to Fairfield." The town had long accepted federal dollars for roads, libraries, and beaches without ceding any local control, but the idea of making this border area less repellant threatened, in this worldview, to invite the poverty and people of color from Bridgeport to creep into Fairfield as another kind of invasive weed. In a special election voters rejected the plan 8,088 to 3,931. Voters also rejected $3 million dollars in free cash that would have erected a youth center along the city border to the north, as well as a developer's plan to build a roller rink near here. Young people of color from Bridgeport were viewed as the source of trouble and drugs. Never mind that by the 1990s, the majority of the drug trade moved the other direction, with suburban buyers free to move where they would on the landscape, and people of color contained. This area was eventually drained and sold off in the 1980s to the car dealerships. Now, within the square half-mile that used to contain the main gateways into Bridgeport, there are six intersections of river and road, railroad and road, rail and river, surface road and highway, and over each intersection, a concrete bridge shades the pavement in darkness.

I crossed the road, heading south from the Tree of Heaven, and stood against a rusty guardrail. The river trickled below, hidden in the brush between two large sites to signal social capital: Land Rover of Milford—located technically in Bridgeport—and a Mercedes Benz dealer and service center in Fairfield, with an Infiniti dealership farther to the west. Beyond the Range Rover building in Bridgeport sat a faceless, gray self-storage building near the highway's curve, offering empty climate-controlled rooms for the overflow of possessions. Most of those places are blight, thrown up by developers to gain significant tax advantages in distressed "enterprise zones" enacted by President Trump in 2018. The credit for dumping tax-free money far outweighs the trickle of income from these facilities, most of which remain unused. Stratford, the town where I live up the coast, attempted to put a moratorium on these faceless non-businesses after several emerged in my neighborhood. Yet we see these as "economic activity," not as earth and sky infested with an invasive presence.

I slipped behind the guardrail and descended amid thistles and goldenrod to the trickle of the creek below, where a metal drain had been installed between the two car dealerships. I walked through reeds along the bank, then crashed uphill and clambered across a collapsed chain link fence. Ahead I spotted the curve where I'd gotten stuck at the railroad tracks. I walked onto the concrete support beneath the railroad bridge. Pigeons cooed, roosting beneath the tracks, a spangle of light from the water reflecting onto the iron and wood above. The rail support was tagged with graffiti, delayed greetings from fellow travelers. I marked lines on my map print-out, finally understanding this ransom note of collaged chunks of river.

Dahlias

By Christine Kalafus

On the nightstand, an empty whisky glass keeps company with the ashy remains of a candle. Last night's hurricane killed the power. Splayed across the wrinkled sheets, Sylvia Plath's *Ariel* lies on top of Virginia Woolf's *Mrs. Dalloway*.

For ticked-off feminist writers, like me, reading Woolf and Plath is required. Especially Plath. It's one of those unspoken literary rules I picked up in graduate school where knowledgeable people walked the Vermont landscape quoting modernist novelists and confessional poets like ancient prophets.

My Bible study is garbage. Rip a teenage girl out of Connecticut and transplant her in Virginia, flooding her Congregationalism with Methodism, who knows what will come up.

At church in the south, I just tried to sing pretty. When that didn't work, I left the sanctuary for the nursery, spending sermons with drooling babies so their parents could take a stab at salvation. Eventually, an opposite Eve, I fled to the garden.

Scattering sheets and books, I fly downstairs, dog at my heels, and whip open the back door. The morning sky is a bright, clear blue.

Dahlias require full sun. Flower heads can be as small and round as a pom-pom and as large and flat as a dinner plate. Tall and strong looking, they deceive. Their hollow stems are not hurricane resistant.

My dahlias arrived from the organic greenhouse tucked in plastic sheaths, nestled in sawdust, not as blooming plants pictured in the catalog, but as dry tubers. Six plants cost one hundred five dollars and ninety-eight cents—money I should have used to buy gasoline for the generator.

Surrounded by storm-tossed branches, sinking bare toes in the dirt, I cup a wet buttercream blossom the size of a saucer with one hand, and with the other, steal a brick from the bed's edge, using it as a wedge, a half-baked support for the dahlia's battered stem.

Initially, I planted them upside down, mistaking tubers for flower pods—stems for roots. Something made me dig the directions out of the trash. The unearthed stems in the late spring sun were like me that first summer in Virginia, diving on a dare into the deep end of the community pool, rising to the surface—enlightened—having seen the bottom with my eyes instead of only feeling it with my feet.

My dog's ears perk up. Coming around the corner is the thundering grab and dump of the weekly garbage truck. Glancing down at my legs, I realize it isn't only shoes I've forgotten, but also pants. But some things are not so easy to forget.

I once contemplated the pressure of a bread knife on my wrist. More than once, I've considered veering into oncoming traffic. Relief from my storms—touchable.

Some of my depressions are noticeable. The one on my forehead took root after running in front of a metal swing set when I was four. The carriage swing, loaded with neighborhood kids, was transformed from a bucket of bolts into a Bugatti. Watching it hurl back and forth, I thought *I can beat it.*

Two identical scars stretch out above my pubic bone, Caesarean portals. Under my right armpit, the spot the surgeon dug for disease-sodden lymph nodes. Across my right breast, a furrow. Other depressions—friends I wore out and discarded, chemo-scarred veins that escape needles, a closed business, a miscarriage—stay hidden. My ghosts.

I am still attached to the idea that I can embrace depression. That I can cradle it as tenderly as a baby, a breast, a book—a scar. Or a fluffy dog.

My English Springer is named Virginia Woof. When I call her, I call myself to the surface. Watch me use an oven. Watch me swim in a river. Watch me write. I escape death if my dog's tail is wagging, if there is a tennis ball in her soft mouth. *I can beat it.*

Hymns fail to lift me up as well as seed packets. As well as my mother's gold bracelet surrounding my wrist. As well as how the featherlight fake crown in the high-end shop felt on my head, and my friend Melissa said *we should wear these when we write*, as well as the poetry and prose of troubled women—as well as a shovel in my palm.

It is said that the color blue, and its association with tears, has existed since antiquity. Whenever he was sad, Zeus would make it rain. Plath died in winter. Woolf, at the very beginning of spring. I chose Dahlias because they are available in every color, except blue.

I live too far north to let them over-winter in the ground. Come October, I'll dig them up, like I am the demi-god of gardening, dust off the dirt, wrap my dahlias in tissue—safe and dry in paper bag sarcophagi—sleeping until spring.

Another Season

By Michael Todd Cohen

You can keep seconds, I want more seasons. I say ten seconds or seventeen seconds or forty-seven seconds and what does that mean? I say Autumn and we're in sweaters and scarves, we're crunching on leaves, inhaling chimney breath. What is an hour alone? Nothing. I say Spring and we're sloshing across fields sodden with rain, lousy with mud and goose shit, tickled with sweetgrass breeze. What even, is, a day? All day long? What is that? 24 hours? 12 hours? 8 hours? Is it when the sun goes down or when the work is done? I say Summer and our bodies are punching heavy-weight waves, we're brining our buzz cuts, and crisping our shoulders, burning our knees; we're into the fruit salad, swatting away flies, we're sitting by fire pits choking on smoke, suckling on bourbons. You say you've been dead eight years now and I keep thinking it's six and what is six years? What is eight? Thirty-two seasons too many, but four is too few. Where is the season called Languor? I say a season called Languor and we're on the patio back home in Massachusetts, watching maple leaf shadows that never move, like our hands never move from the stone they make together. Where is the season called Ecstasy? When all we do is fuck and never cum? Or the season called Gluttor? Elator? Or Wanderning? And you say you've been dead six years? No, that's not right. It's eight. I say Winter and we're climbing over dirty street corner snow drifts, ducking into jazz bars playing hot hiss steam pipe symphonies, we're tucking into chicken pot pie, into down comforters, into shared dreams from which you never wake.

Reclaiming My Name

By Vesna Jaksic Lowe

I'm clutching a carry-on at an Air Canada check-in kiosk, my palms sweating as the agent taps on the keyboard, her red nails mirroring her lipstick. I want her to look up and hand me that magic strip of white paper, but her gaze is affixed to the screen in front of her.

"It doesn't match," she says in the flat voice of an authoritarian figure exercising her power. She doesn't look at me, but points her manicured finger at my passport, then the boarding pass. Her red nails hover above the letters like a teacher's pen. My teeth clench and throat tightens, but I summon my patience. For the second time, I explain that I do not have a middle name. One half of my two-part last name was wrongly dropped in the middle name box.

The Croatian portion of my last name—Jaksic—often gets demoted to a middle name, discarded, or reduced to its first initial, the remaining five letters tossed aside because of some bureaucrat's assumptions, laziness, or both. The American part of my last name— Lowe—is the only one left standing. And with that, so much of who I am perishes: my home country of Croatia, my beautiful childhood by the Adriatic Sea, and my father's deep roots in our medieval walled city of Dubrovnik.

They perish because of careless administrators, ignorant robots, or computers confused about foreign married names. But over and over, I'm forced to reclaim my last name, which is, of course, not just about six letters. It's about family, identity, roots. It carries my history and my background. As Sahaj Kaur Kohli, creator of Brown Girl Therapy and advice columnist for *The Washington Post,* said, "Our names are an extension of our identities and root us in our family cultures and histories. For many, they serve as a core representation of where we are from. Names hold meaning, pride, strength and courage, and they deserve to be honored."

I can't help but think these mistakes are also about patriarchal systems that refuse to accommodate women who keep their names after marriage. My name is a part of me, and I want it back, whether it's on my boarding pass, library card, or Verizon bill.

I was born and raised in Yugoslavia, and left with my family just before a series of civil wars shattered the country. I have documents from four countries—Serbia, where I was born; Croatia, where I grew up; Canada, where I emigrated; and the United States, where I now live. I am always renewing some soon-to-be expired ID, rummaging through a shoebox in the bedroom closet for translations of my birth certificate, sifting through an alphabet soup of immigration visas before filling out yet another form to prove my existence—begging some broken government for permission to belong. I worry I'll miss a deadline that keeps my humanity up-to-date, that I'll expire, be erased from some database that lets me work, lets me travel, lets me exist. That instead of being put in the wrong box, there won't be a box for me.

My name and background are always undergoing scrutiny, leading to additional lines at airports, calls for supervisors at the DMV, and error messages in online applications. But there is deep privilege connected to my box of passports resembling a model UN. I am not stateless, nor do I live in fear like many people who are undocumented. My papers are inseparable from my white skin, which has shielded me from racism and discrimination at the airport, at work, on the road, at the park, in my home.

I had a job offer rescinded once when my work visa didn't arrive in time, have not been eligible for countless opportunities as a non-U.S. citizen, and often get separated from my American husband and daughter at airports. My white immigrant body may have to deal with inconvenience and stress, but that is a world away from the terror and violence unleashed on the 2" x 2" Black and brown faces in passport books.

At the airport kiosk, I explain to the Air Canada agent again that "J" is not a middle initial because I do not have a middle name. I inform her that many Croats don't have a middle name, as if my international identity warrants an explanation. I occupy the roles of translator and educator, like so many immigrants do when interacting with authorities. By now, I am used to having to explain myself, whether it's to an airline agent, an immigration officer, or a Starbucks barista. I do it all bearing a fake smile, that popular tool in an immigrant's toolbox used to demonstrate our compliance and disguise our fears. We know how to make ourselves more quiet, smaller, and invisible. We understand the unwritten rules about engaging with officials while being an immigrant.

The agent eventually hands me the boarding pass. "Just this time," she says with furrowed eyebrows, as if she did me a favor over a mistake I did not make. "Next time, please don't put your middle name in the last name box."

"I don't have a..." I start, then grab the boarding pass and walk away. "Forget it..."

I rush to the gate and text my husband. "The thing with my last name happened again. I barely made the flight!" He responds with a sad emoji. He's used to me complaining about neighbors calling me "Mrs. Lowe," e-invites addressed to "The Lowes," and family Christmas cards bearing only his last name.

I recall a day I had to e-mail my insurance agent because once again, he had chopped my name on my car insurance card, stripping it down to its American skeleton. To the simple. The familiar. The acceptable. I took far too long to draft a message to him because I didn't want to piss off Tripp, the Connecticut insurance agent, so I typed "I'm sorry" and described that I needed my name corrected because I had paperwork issues at the DMV.

Sitting behind a plexiglass screen, the DMV agent had compared the shortened version of my name on my insurance card with other documents. "Your last name doesn't match," she said. "Yeah, I know," I said exasperated, then went home and e-mailed the insurance agent. As the cursor blinked over my second "sorry," my right pinkie reached toward the delete button and tapped five times. *Why I am sorry for someone else's mistake? Why do I need to justify that I deserve every syllable of my name? Why am I apologizing for the only thing I've owned since birth?*

These are not the only times my name has undergone a transformation. When my family emigrated from Yugoslavia to Canada, we dropped the accents that sat atop the letters S and C in our last name—Jakšić—turning them into "ch" and "sh" sounds. I was 13 and don't recall my parents, two sisters or me giving it much thought. We left on the brink of war—there were bigger things to worry about. We probably shaved the accents off because English does not have these letters in its alphabet, so it made getting an avalanche of new documents in a new country and language a little easier. Maybe we tried to smooth out our complex past by flattening the sounds in our name. We replaced the hard European consonants with their English counterparts, which rolled off the tongue more easily.

Somewhere on that one-way cross-Atlantic flight to Toronto, we let those two accents drift away. They became sacrifices in our migrant journey, along with the piggy-tailed stuffed doll I couldn't take with me and the turquoise terry cloth blanket I loved sleeping with. The five of us stuffed our lives into five suitcases—we couldn't take everything. The accents became another thing we could do without, another victim of our quest to integrate in a new culture. Like so many immigrants, we focused on adapting in our new home country and didn't think about the costs of assimilation. We focused on acquiring new things—a new language, a new job, new friends. Now, as an adult, I think about the losses that came with that—distancing myself from my mother tongue, my friends back home, my culture.

I've spent most of my life with those two pieces missing from my name, altering its spelling and pronunciation. I became a teenager and an immigrant in the same year, so I was busy trying to blend in and sound like my Canadian peers. To shed my Eastern European accent and fit in with my eighth-grade classmates, I surrendered the Croatian accents in my name. *They can pronounce it better like this*, I thought. *It sounds cooler in English.* I worried about how to make it easier for others to say my name, not about why I felt othered by my name. I justified. I explained.

In a way, I did the same thing as the Air Canada ticket agent and the Connecticut insurance guy. I covered up my foreignness, hid my otherness, and erased myself. I took the easy way out by choosing the version that was simpler to say and didn't elicit questions about my roots.

And now that I'm in my forties and living in a United States that demonizes immigrants, I think about those tiny diagonal lines that ceased existing on top of one moon-shaped letter and one swirly letter. I think about how as soon as we landed in a new country and unpacked our suitcases, we embodied our role of "good immigrants" by letting go of our accents. And I wish that my teenage self had the strength to hold on to them, to embrace them in her skinny, insecure body. And that it wouldn't take decades for me to gather enough courage to insist that my name be treated correctly, whether at an airport, DMV counter, or on a Christmas card. I wish I'd understood that for me to survive, I didn't have to let the accents go.

Sent Away

By Gabi Coatsworth

My pregnant mother had driven us there in the second-hand Hillman Minx that would soon be too small for our growing family. When we tumbled out of the back seat, she explained—for the tenth time at least—that we would only be here for a few weeks over the summer. I was four years old, the twins Jane and Kay were six, and I had a sinking feeling as our car rolled to a stop in the driveway of a Victorian Gothic country house, Hawson Court, in deepest Devon, England. Madame Małkowska, founder of the girl scouts in Poland before the war, ran a summer camp for Polish children there. Since my father was Polish, we qualified.

Temporarily placing children in a home like this was not uncommon after World War II, and could happen for many reasons.

Our father had been ill and was now recovering in a convalescent home not far away in Torquay, a popular resort because of its sunny location and fresh sea air. So we'd be on a kind of vacation while Daddy got better.

"It'll be fun, you'll see," said Mummy, blowing her nose on a handkerchief. Her eyes looked red. She grabbed my hand and the Twins clung to each other as we walked up to the huge oak door where she tugged at the bellpull, which startled us with its ominous clang. As the sound died away, it was replaced by the clack of feet in heavy shoes approaching the door from the other side. I tried to hide behind the skirt of my mother's maternity smock, as if to gain courage by osmosis. Perhaps no one would notice me and I'd be able to sneak into the car and go home.

The door swung open, giving us our first sight of Madame Małkowska. Probably in her sixties, she was an accumulation of rigid lines. Her completely straight salt-and-pepper hair was cropped into a vicious bob, parted on one side, with a hairgrip that pinned the longer side back, hiding the top of her forehead. Her face was scrubbed and pale, and her dress, a battleship gray color, fell with absolutely no curves whatsoever to below her knees, where her sturdy legs were encased in thick lisle stockings, even though it was a beautiful day in early summer. Madame's shoes filled me with dread, for they reminded me of Daddy's army shoes, the ones at the back of the wardrobe. They went with the uniform that he never wore. Were we going to be in the army?

Something very like it, as it turned out.

Madame's thin-lipped smile made me grab another handful of my mother's dress and twist it around my small fist, until she reached down and carefully disengaged my hand. She straightened up as the woman greeted her in Polish. I could say a few words and understood more, so I tried to follow along as my mother, an Englishwoman, made small talk.

"Say hello to Mme. Małkowska. Po polsku."

"Dzień dobry, Pani," we murmured.

Looking past Madame's solid form, I could make out a shadowy hall, with a sweeping oak staircase running up one side. The only light came from behind us, as it seeped into the hallway from outside. I felt like a timid elf entering the menacing cavern of a giant.

"You had better come inside," said Mme. Małkowska.

We trudged into the gloom and stood on the cold red-and-yellow tiled floor, waiting.

"Marula will bring the cases," said Madame, indicating a bespectacled woman who'd appeared from the depths of the house. She wasn't at all pretty, but she smiled kindly at me, revealing uneven teeth. I felt a little better. I liked the way her hair was braided into a kind of crown around her head. Her face had no trace of makeup, but I inhaled a reassuringly normal smell of Sunlight kitchen soap as she squeezed past us, taking the warmth with her.

We climbed the long staircase to the upper floor.

"The girls will sleep here," said Madame, only it sounded like "slip here."

We stared at the light but chilly room that contained seven metal bedsteads jammed against the walls. Mme. Małkowska explained the system to Mummy.

"The children get up at six o'clock every morning. Then they take their toothbrush and paste and a towel and come here." She led us to the bathroom, which stretched before us, its cracked linoleum still showing signs of the original pattern. To the left stood an enameled bathtub on legs. Straight ahead a window overlooked the garden where we could see other children playing.

"Here all children bathe every day before they dress. A daily bath is necessary for the wellness."

Mummy nodded, but I knew that her recipe for maintaining our well-being was another Polish saying she'd learned: Laughter is health.

"They wear usual clothing except for Sunday, when, of course, we go to Mass. Then they must wear their best dress."

"They have a dress each. So, are they allowed..."

"I have not finished yet, Mrs. Grajnert. They have their own prayer books?"

"Well, they're only four and six years old," she began, "so..."

"Never mind. The small one cannot read yet anyway." Mummy did not bother to contradict her. I knew how to read; it was the Twins who had trouble making out words on the page.

The breeze from the bathroom window moved Mummy's hair across her brow, and she brushed it away.

"And here," Mme. Małkowska said, unlocking the doors of a tall wooden cupboard, "is where I keep sweet things."

We stared, intrigued. Confectionery was rationed at home, not just by Mummy but in the shops, too, because of the war. This cabinet contained more sweets than we'd ever seen.

"The children are allowed two on Sundays after lunch." Our interest turned to disappointment. At home, Mummy allowed us something sugary every day. "So, if you will hand me whatever you have brought for the girls, I will put them away."

Mummy pulled a small package of fruit drops and three rolls of Polo mints from her shoulder bag and handed them over. She didn't look very happy. Mme. Małkowska locked the door of the cupboard, put the key in her pocket, and headed downstairs.

Back in the hall, she escorted us into a sunny room containing a large table, surrounded by several chairs.

"Meals are in here, and through here, is the playroom."

This was larger than the dining room, with windows shadowed by tall butterfly bushes that grew outside. The light filtering in gave the room a greenish tinge that made it seem a little sad. Though the space was deserted, under the window seat lay a collection of toys, interesting because they were new to me. I scanned the battered wooden train set, the small model cars parked in straight lines, and the row of faded dolls on parade along the wall. I could even see a few picture books on a shelf. Maybe this place would be bearable after all.

Mme. Małkowska was speaking again.

"I think it is time for you to leave now, Mrs. Grajnert." My mother's smile faded. "The children will be having excellent time here, won't you, girls?" We stood silent.

"All will be good, Mrs. Grajnert," repeated Mme. Małkowska. "It is better if you go—if not, the more harder it will be. And you will not want to set a bad example, of course." Her beady eyes bored into my mother's.

"You're right, I suppose," said Mummy in a funny voice. In the frigid hall, she leaned down to look into our faces.

"Remember girls," she blinked rather rapidly, "Daddy and I will be coming to fetch you soon—in a week or so. And we'll write, I promise."

She kissed Jane and Kay and lowered herself to crouch in front of me. I flung myself at her and grabbed her around the neck as hard as I could.

"Mummy, please don't go." I sobbed into her collar. "Don't leave me here."

My mother gulped.

"Gabi, darling, you'll be with the Twins, so you won't be alone. You can take care of each other, until we come for you. It's just that Daddy has to stay in a hospital for a while so he can get better."

"He's already been in a hospital, he must be better now," I insisted.

"This is a different place, darling, and he needs a bit more rest before he's quite well again."

She hugged me fiercely, and I hoped that meant that she would keep on hugging me and take me with her, away from here. But she picked me up, kissed me once more, and set me down. She took out her handkerchief and gently wiped our eyes.

"Be brave girls," she tried to sound encouraging. "It won't be long."

She blew her nose, and walked over to the car. Seating herself awkwardly in the driver's seat, she switched on the engine, and turned her face to us with a strained attempt at a smile. She waved, then bit her lip, and drove off quickly, as we watched her disappear behind the overgrown rhododendrons that lined the drive.

Lying in bed that evening, I heard the Twins talking softly. They had always had each other for company, and as babies, even had their own language. But I didn't feel so alone with them around.

In the gloom of the bedroom, I couldn't make out exactly where they were.

"Kay, where are you?" I whispered.

"Over here, in the corner."

"I think it's horrible here, and I want to go home."

"We do too," answered Jane. Her natural cheerfulness came through. "At least you've got Mish, and we've got our rag dolls."

I clutched my teddy harder, and drank in his familiar, comforting smell.

"Be quiet," a Polish girl hissed from another bed. "We're not allowed to speak now."

I ignored the warning.

"Is Daddy going to be all right?"

"Who is that still talking?" came Madame's voice from the landing.

"Me, Madame."

"Gabriella, there is silence here after lights out. You must learn to obey orders, or you will be in trouble."

Madame's ponderous footsteps retreated down the stairs.

"'Night, 'night, Twins."

"See you in the morning, Gabi."

That's what Mummy always said when she tucked us in. I turned over, holding Mish even more tightly, and buried my face in his fur.

We woke early the next morning at the sound of a bell ringing nearby.

"Quickly, girls and boys, bring your towel and toothbrush with you."

Shoving our feet into the dark red felt slippers our mother had made for us, we shuffled into the bathroom behind the other children. It was cool in there—cold even, because of the wind blowing through the open window. Mme. Małkowska seemed to read my mind.

"Wonderful fresh air. It's the best thing for young bodies. Now take off your night clothes."

The Twins and I stared at each other, shocked.

"She doesn't mean here, does she?" I muttered to the girl next to me. Her expression registered nothing. I said it again in Polish.

"Oh yes, we have to bathe now. It will harden us."

The little girl looked frail compared with our sturdy forms. I didn't need to be hardened, I decided. Definitely not, if I had to take my pajamas off in front of everyone. My sisters hung back behind me,

24

with identical anxious expressions. At that moment a firm hand gripped my shoulder.

"Come along, take them off."

My resolution crumbled. Madame loomed above us, and the others were starting to undress. The bath tap stopped running, with about two inches of water in the bottom of the old-fashioned tub. I wondered how the brown stains had got onto the enamel, but I didn't really want to know.

"Kasia, you first. In you go...lie down, that's right...now roll over, and...out. And next!"

I watched, frozen, as the children climbed into the bath one by one and, with audible gasps, lay down, rolled over in the water, and then clambered out, grabbing their towels. Now for my turn. That woman intended to make me get into the same water that all the others had been in.

"I can't. I don't want to." I could feel the tears welling up.

"You want to be a scout, don't you? Scouts must to be tough. Get in!"

If being a scout meant being like Madame, I didn't want to be one, ever. But I knew she would make me do it, so I took a deep breath and hopped in. The bathwater was icy—I shuddered.

"It's cold," I whimpered, half crouching in the bath, not wanting the others to see me rolling over.

"Naturally," came the stern reply. "Because warm water makes people soft."

My mother's frequent reminders when giving us horrid-tasting medicine came back to me. "The quicker you take it, the quicker it will be over."

I turned over and scrambled up, forgetting the audience in my haste to get out again.

Safely on the bathmat, I wrapped as much of myself as I could in my towel, and stood dripping water and shivering with the others until everyone had "bathed."

I wanted to cry, but I knew one thing. Madame would not be kind to anyone who showed weakness. Perhaps this was what she meant by being hardened. I clenched my chattering teeth and vowed she would not win.

Back in the bedroom, our clothes lay ready on the end of each bed.

Marula, the help, had supervised us the night before as we laid out our things for the morning. She was back now, offering to brush our hair.

I grimaced as she scraped the hair back from my forehead, wrapped an elastic band around it, then wove a ribbon through, but the final effect in the mirror surprised me. I resembled all the other little Polish girls, except, of course, that my hair was red. Meanwhile, the Twins' blond curls refused to be flattened by the brush, and fluffed around their heads like unruly haloes.

"Oh, thank you, Marula. I look so nice."

"Is nothing to thank me for. I like make hair good. Now is time for breakfast."

In the dining room, seated opposite me, Madame checked to make sure everyone had a napkin, and was ready to eat. I reached my hand forward, but a girl next to me nudged my elbow and indicated Madame with a nod. She sat ramrod straight with her hands together and was starting to pray—a long prayer in Polish that I didn't know. I folded my hands too and waited.

"Marula, pour out some milk for the children," ordered Madame.

I liked milk, so I picked up my mug eagerly and took a swig. But one swallow, and I wanted to spit it out. It smelled strange and tasted worse.

"Gabriella—drink up correctly," came Madame's voice.

But I couldn't and I wouldn't.

"That's not right," I blurted out. "Is it?" I appealed to the Twins. They shook their heads solemnly.

"Nonsense. That's very good milk, and still warm from the goat."

26

Goat? I shuddered.

"Drink it up right now. You don't want me to tell your mother you are wasting food, do you?"

Of course not. My mother worried enough. Besides, she didn't let us leave food on our plates either.

After breakfast, we had chores to do. Mine was to take care of the long staircase with a landing halfway up, which needed to be waxed and polished once a week. Marula showed me how to apply the lavender-scented floor wax—the smell of it repelled me for years after. I had to rub it in, making sure not to miss any corner, and then polish the stairs to a shine with old rags, until they passed Madame's inspection.

After chores, we played outside or in the playroom, or Madame taught us Polish songs about being brave soldiers and dying for our fatherland. Though I was only four, I didn't want to be a brave soldier. That was for people like my mother, who had been in the army during the war. Her uniform hung in the wardrobe alongside my father's.

"Does everyone have to die for their fatherland?" I asked one day that week, worried about my father. He'd survived the war but was sick now because of it.

"Many have died already, many, many..." said Madame, and she stared off into the distance.

I noticed that people who'd been in the War did that sometimes. My mother said it was better not to ask about it, though occasionally, once we'd brushed our teeth and were tucked into bed, she and my father would tell us about their wartime experiences. No one perished in their stories, which were full of miraculous escapes and hilarious anecdotes.

Mme. Małkowska was clapping her hands to get our attention and the memory of those bedtimes vanished with the sound.

"Time to play outside now, children."

She led us all through a door at the back and into a garden with a plot of grass, rather worn in places from the running of small feet. I glanced across the grass, mesmerized by the view beyond the garden, which reminded me of the pictures in my Blackberry Farm book, with mauve hills and green fields that rolled away in the distance. Because the garden itself sloped downward, it appeared to have no finite boundary, but to be cut away like a cliff top some way from where we were standing.

This place was much too vast for me.

I longed for the confining safety of our back-garden fence at home, which successfully kept us separated from our neighbors but provided no hindrance at all to the cats that would come by in search of milk. Hedgehogs found their way in, too, and even the occasional tortoise. We loved these tortoises and the way they appeared from nowhere. We'd come across them enthusiastically eating Daddy's carefully planted lettuces. They never ran away when they realized we were nearby but placidly allowed themselves to be picked up and brought to the kitchen door to be shown to our mother, who would give them cabbage leaves to eat. Once, Daddy made us laugh by taking the garden hose and, holding a tortoise aloft, running water over its head and through its shell. To our amazement, it started swimming, as naturally as if it had been in a pond.

I couldn't see any animals here.

On Sundays, we were taken to Buckfast Abbey for Mass, sung by black-robed Benedictine monks. Perhaps as a reward, on certain afternoons we went for walks, following Madame as she strode ahead, with Marula bringing up the rear, to make sure no one dawdled behind. The route I visualize in my memory took us along country lanes with a little brook running to one side. I stopped to drink some water in my cupped hand, because I was thirsty, and I'd heard of children doing this in books. Madame shouted at me. "This water is dirty! Dirty! You will die, I expect."

I said fervent prayers for the next few nights. I always prayed that my father would get better. And that soon my mother would arrive to pick me and the Twins up to take us home. Now I prayed and waited, terrified I would die from a gulp of water before I could be rescued. But as I continued to wake every morning, I forgot about my impending death. Madame Małkowska, though, I'd never forget. My hatred for her became deep and unforgiving, and my fear of being left with her—or anyone like her—made me resolve to be incredibly good when we returned home. I wouldn't risk my parents sending me away again.

My Body Attacks Itself

By Joan Sidney

STORRS, CONNECTICUT, June 11, 2021

My weekend personal care assistant (PCA) struggles to pull off my left compression stocking, scraping my ankle. Instantly, my leg jerks up to my chest. In her three years helping me live with multiple sclerosis (MS), this might be the first time she inadvertently bruises my ankle, which causes painful spasms. But I have no worries as she proceeds to smear layers of topical medical marijuana from toe to thigh. Besides, I just took a combo of both allopathic and homeopathic bed meds to relax my muscles. She transfers me to bed and proceeds to float my legs on the usual three pillows; I become the princess and the pea. But each time she gently pulls my left leg in place, it spasms painfully up to my chest. I look at myself, my left leg bent and splayed on top of the pillows. Again and again, she attempts to reposition my leg. Again and again, my leg jerks back in painful protest. It's been decades since my last exacerbation, and with one last touch of her fingers, the leg spasms shoot me back to 1995 in Lyon, France.

LYON, SPRING 1995

I've been willing to try any non-invasive treatment available to find a cure for my MS. Sensing my desperation, my homeopath's receptionist puts me in touch with Philippe, a patient who insists I see the practitioner who "cured" him. How? He doesn't say, nor do I ask. Not my typical behavior, but I trust this referral from my medical office even if it has nothing to do with my doctor.

30

"Dr. Odru sees only people with incurable illnesses, Thursday to Sunday from four to midnight. No appointments, so it's a long wait," Philippe warns. "No Sécu, bring cash."

Late Saturday afternoon, my husband Stu drives us to Lyon and finds a parking spot around the corner. I'm excited and optimistic, especially when I enter the waiting room and see that Philippe is right. Not an empty seat in this bare-walled, windowless room which smells of sweat. Fortunately, I sit on my rolling walker's seat while Stu leans against the wall behind me. We listen to patients share stories of how traditional medicine has abandoned them, and of Dr. Odru's ongoing office treatments of their formerly "incurable" cancers and other serious illnesses. The door opens. A stocky, medium-height, middle-aged man calls for the next person. No sign of the previous patient. Finally, after hours of waiting, it's my turn. Instead of emptying out, the seats are filled with new people, each face mirroring my optimism. There's no way they'll be gone by midnight.

We step through the door into a small room whose only furniture is a halogen floor lamp and a treatment table. It's too dark to see anything through the floor to ceiling windows.

"Take off your shirt and lie on your belly across the table," Odru says, after listening to why I've come. Braless and half-naked, I let Stu position me perpendicular to the table. Odru sprays something sweet-smelling and slippery up and down my back. With the flat palm of his right hand, he scrapes and spreads my vertebrae. I bite my lower lip to avoid screaming from pain. Never did a treatment hurt like this. I close my eyes and go inside my body, watching my T-cells back away from the myelin sheaths of my nerve cells.

When I open my eyes much later, Odru says, "Come back in a month," as he helps me off the table. "Don't shock your body."

I'm not sure what that means, but it's late, we're exhausted—we don't ask. Stu helps me with my shirt and pays Odru the equivalent of $80 dollars. Odru lets us out through the French doors—not what I thought were windows—into the building's courtyard, where he tells us to park next time. Now I know why patients seemed to disappear after treatment.

Ninety minutes later, I practically race up the thirteen uneven stone steps leading to our one-bedroom mountain rental. No need for ski poles or rolling walker anymore, obviously Jean-Marie Odru is the real deal. A few more treatments and this incurable disease will be history. For sure, Blue Cross/Blue Shield will be happy to reimburse me.

Although I get up in pain the next morning after a sleepless night on my stomach, surprised still to need my rolling walker for support, how can I not believe in Odru? Despite the pain, the remission—though temporary—was real. Next time, I'll ask him how to make it last.

I'm shocked when Pierre, my acupuncturist, asks a few days later, "What happened to your back? Who burned you? It's red and blistered."

"A few more treatments and I, like Philippe, will be cured," I tell Pierre.

He shakes his head in warning. Did I ever see him scowl before?

Again and again, I return to Odru's office. I knock at his outer door. Instead of his waiting room, he lets us sit in the other treatment room. Hours always pass. After treatment, I always effortlessly climb the stairs to our apartment. Why does that miracle last only a few hours? I want to ask but am afraid to question this non-traditional doctor and possibly be turned away. Not questioning is atypical for me, but so are Odru's methods and results, even though the results are temporary—for now.

Why don't I call Philippe to compare notes, or even to meet? From my first two exacerbations, I know about MS's unpredictability. Each time after resting a few months, my disease went into remission. Maybe that happened to Philippe. Maybe it had nothing to do with Odru. But I believe in him—or need to—and don't back off.

LA PISCINE, ST. MARTIN D'URIAGE, JUNE 1ˢᵗ, 1995

"Stop! The water's too cold," the *maître nageur* warns. Later he will tell us nobody has come to swim yet. If only we had listened.

"No," Stu says. "Cold water helps Joan. It gives her a remission." True, that's the way it's always been both for me and others with MS. Years ago, my friend Chris told me about seeing people with MS at the beach. "They practically crawled to the water. After swimming, they walked normally. I did, too," Chris said.

But aside from fatigue, without sweatshirt and sweatpants, I feel chilled on this gray day. I dive in, stroke quickly back and forth across the pool, unable to warm up. Instead of the usual remission, my muscles relaxing, my body becoming stronger, I feel as if someone stole my old body. My legs refuse to kick, so I stroke and shiver. Eventually, I give up and try to climb out of the pool, but my legs collapse at the bottom step. The *maître nageur* sees, bends down and lifts me out of the water. He rubs me vigorously with my towel. My left knee is in spasm up to my breast. Holding on to my rolling walker, I hop to the hot shower but can't warm up. Nor does hot tea help.

The next afternoon we drive to Lyon.

"I told you not to shock your body," Odru says, blaming me for my predicament. I hate when a doctor blames the patient, especially if I'm the patient.

"I told you I reversed your illness," he says, his voice getting louder.

"Put your wife on the table," he tells Stu, not looking at me.

Despite his painful treatment, my left leg doesn't loosen its grip. Will it ever come back down? If Odru can't undo what he caused to happen, who can?

For weeks nothing helps: not physical therapy, not acupuncture, not yoga. With my mother's imminent visit and Stu's upcoming lecture trip to Newcastle, I need to find a neurologist. He sends me to Clinique Belledonne, where twenty-three years before, our youngest son, Larry, was born. The neurologist orders a daily infusion of Solumedrol—although I rarely even take an aspirin for a headache or fever. Desperate, I agree to it and a week of rest. This time I return without a newborn, but at least my leg has come down to normal. "The rest probably did as much as the Solumedrol," the neurologist said.

But rest has never been on my to-do list.

PRAYER MEETING, JULY 1995

At supper I tell Mom about tomorrow's trip. A friend wants me to meet an important priest, whose reputation as a miracle healer has made him Christ-like. But instead of her usual approval, my mild-mannered mom is furious.

"Joanie, are you crazy? Leaving in the middle of the night to see a charlatan."

"Why do you call him 'a charlatan'? What do you know about him that I should know?"

How does she know who could or could not heal me? Is she just too Jewish to believe in a priest?

"I don't want to upset you, Joanie. I've always helped you pay for treatments your insurance won't cover, but if nothing you've tried has helped, why should this meshugenah be different?"

"Mom, you know I can't give up. Someone, somewhere, will heal me, I just need to find that someone."

I stretch out my arms and pull her close as tears drip down our cheeks.

At 4 a.m. with Colette Pilon, my landlord and close friend, I leave for a day of prayer meetings more than four hours away.

By the time we arrive, the field overflows with parked cars. We head to a stage filled with speakers but are directed to a huge tent for *les grandes malades*. Compared to those on stretchers and wheelchairs, I am almost healthy. But I've come to meet this priest and want to feel his hands heal me. If he's Christ's reincarnation, why shouldn't he be happy to heal another Jew?

Colette and I sneak out of the tent to hear those on-stage giving testimony, praising the priest's healing. Then, in flowing white robes, the priest appears. Enormous applause. As though on cue, he picks people from the front row to come on stage. Each one complains of an invisible illness. The priest puts his hands on each one's head, mumbles a prayer, dismisses him or her as *guéri*.

Hours go by with no chance of me or any unchosen others getting near the priest. I admit to myself that Mom was right. Despite what my friend thought, this was a set-up. The priest's agenda has veered from pretend healing to a diatribe against birth control and abortion. The sun's heat sends us back to the tent only to find a mass of heartbroken, ill people weeping.

Enough! We head to the car. I look back at the stage and, instead of a priest, I see an actor hypnotizing his audience with clichéd words. As always, I'm grateful to Colette for her patience and love. We agree not to breathe a word of our experience to Mom. No need for her lecture. At 53, I'm entitled to make my own mistakes. But as we drive past a field of lavender, its scent filling our nostrils, I am torn between the beauty of this world and the ugliness of human nature, as well as the stupidity of people to let one ordinary man with an enormous ego become godlike at the expense of the ill.

CEREBÈRE, SEPTEMBER 1995

After a summer of painful spasms—once the Solumedrol wore off my left knee returned to kissing my breast. Stu helps me pack for a month at Cerebère, a rehab center at Centre Cap Peyrefite, near the Spanish border on the Mediterranean. Because of my chronic illness, French socialized medicine put me in the category of *grande malade*. In contrast to American medical insurance, Sécurité Sociale transports me first class by taxi and pays for all of my medical expenses. My driver tells me, "This trip costs $500 each way."

Because I am still on the Kousmine diet, organic-vegetarian, I bring my own food for the first two weeks, knowing Stu will visit at the half-time mark with fresh organic veggies. Working with a specialized dietician in Grenoble, I believe I am on the right track. No way would I take a month off and undo my efforts. Though the dining room food looks fine, mine looks better, especially since it's free of toxins. Nor do I miss meat.

The next morning a physiatrist, with a Polish name, examines me and sets up my care routine. He prescribes a minimal dose a day of the classic muscle relaxer Lioresol (Baclofen), to calm my spasms and bring down my knee. But in these days—except for that one Solumedrol week—I refuse to take allopathic meds, only homeopathics. "The physical therapists can't stretch your leg without Lioresol. You'll get a contracture," the physiatrist warns. I have no idea what he's talking about, nor do I ask.

After taking Lioresol for two days, I fall asleep in the afternoon, missing my crafts activity, painting on silk—my first wall-hanging is a hot-air balloon that I'll mail to Mom—and I refuse to continue. "Lioresol will help you," the physiatrist says, "this is the ideal place to try it out." "I'm Polish and stubborn, too," I say, as if we are competing.

I think I know better because I went to the Upledger Institute for Brain and Spinal Cord Disorders twice in 1992, where all week their experienced physical therapists used CranioSacral therapy (CST) to help my body heal itself. It's a gentle, hands-on method of evaluating and treating the patient by releasing restrictions in the cranial system. This helps the central nervous system function better. CST either spoiled or brainwashed me. After Upledger, I didn't want conventional physical therapy.

Only in hindsight do I realize the physiatrist's right. His staff of newly-certified traveling PTs don't know CST, and after a few minutes of stretching without Lioresol, my hamstrings spasm, and the PTs don't know how to help me. This defeats the reason I am here. Nonetheless, instead of giving both Lioresol and the PTs a fair chance, I revel in my vacation. Mornings I swim laps with another patient in the indoor pool, with floor to ceiling windows facing the Mediterranean. Afternoons I hop down to the seaside with my rolling walker, admiring the calm blue waters and reading. Instead of PT, I work out between the parallel bars, which does nothing to bring down my left leg. Two days a week I take driving lessons on a car with hand controls. What an opportunity to drive the narrow, winding roads of this beach town!

FALL 1995

I return to our Venon apartment in time to start my dream job at the Université de Grenoble III: Maître de Langue Étrangère. Jean Dérioz, the English Department Head, has given me the most manageable full-time schedule possible. I teach the first-ever semester-long creative writing class, also a conversational English lab class, and, in addition, each week I read and record articles of my choosing from the *International Herald Tribune* for a blind student. But the excitement of preparation and teaching, the joy of French university life, vies with my painful spasticity.

After his University of Connecticut fall semester finals, my son Larry arrives with my L.L.Bean order, two pair of winter slacks. He accompanies me to my conversation course. The female-dominated group responds to the feminist text I assigned, demolishing Larry and the lone male student. In a minute my students are gone when the class ends. But before I can wheel out from under the desk, my left leg spasms up, jamming me in place. I scream in pain. Larry massages my leg and gently frees me from the desk.

I hate this wake-up call.

I don't want to leave my best job ever. I don't want to trade Maître de Langue Étrangère for adjunct at a local Connecticut university. I don't want to leave my friends in this magical mountain village, where neighbors knock at my door and stay for *tisane*. No appointments necessary, unlike Storrs, where no one just drops by. But I can't stay. My taxi driver has already warned me that he'll be unable to wheel me up and down the thirteen uneven stone steps when winter weather comes. Nor has Stu been able to find anyone else with whom to job-swap spring semester. If he leaves, I can no longer stay alone.

Stu and I sit on the living room sofa looking from one to the other, unable to come up with a viable alternative. After a while, I watch the sun sink into the crevice between two mountain peaks. Below, the lights of Grenoble twinkle on.

THE RETURN, JANUARY 1996

Old friends load us and our belongings into their Renault station wagon and drive us 90 minutes to the Geneva Airport. "When will you visit?" I ask, already missing them.

"Maybe next summer, if I can arrange a Franco-American student exchange."

"I'll look forward to seeing you," I say, trying to smile.

They accompany us to the Swiss Air check-in counter, where the agent insists on charging us so much for our many suitcases that it comes to the price of another ticket. Instead of arguing with her, I ask to speak with her manager. Fortunately, our travel agent had arranged for us to avoid extra baggage charges, so we kiss our friends, *à bientôt,* and board the jumbo jet.

I can't stop crying. A flight attendant attempts to console me.

"What's wrong? How can I help?" he asks, taking my hand.

"I don't want to leave France," I say, blowing my nose.

"You'll be back. I can tell."

I thank him and fall asleep.

COLUMBIA, CONNECTICUT, SEPTEMBER 7, 2020

Kirsten, my therapeutic riding instructor, slips a lift sling under my butt, hooks the cords onto the cradle, presses the remote, and swings me into the saddle. "Such a beautiful day," she says. "If you're strong enough, let's try the trail." Immediately my left leg stiffens, shoots up. I'm not sure what scares me most about the trail I've never explored. The steep descent or ascent she's described? If I'm unsteady in the flat arena, struggling to stay erect, it'll be more difficult to manage going down, than up the trail. Damn contracture that haunts my life.

But on that day and all through the winter-spring riding sessions, I tackle the trail in good weather, reaching to ring the bell and even toss a ball into the trailside hoop. At the same time, I am riding in Camargue with my friends; Camargue, the home of wild horses; also the flamingoes' mating grounds to which they return each year. Twice we camped on the beach in their rented RV. I still hear strangers knocking on the door during a storm, warning us to move, that the water was getting close.

As I ride up Monster Hill, "Breathe deep," Kirsten says. "Let the air steady your pelvis and your core. Keep your eyes on the top of the trees."

And I do.

Child of Immigrants

By Michelle Hernandez

After "Girl" by Jamaica Kincaid

Say your name the way you want it to be said; live to please yourself, don't worry about being a stereotype or statistic; people are judgmental, and their opinions don't matter unless you let them count; you don't have to announce where you're from all the time; don't feel the need to share your family history to be validated by others; know that saving money is a luxury; go to school, get that diploma, bachelor's and master's degrees (and a Ph.D. to be extra); know that the English language is not a measurement of intelligence; don't be sorry, do better; people may feel challenged by you because you're different; people may treat you differently because you're different; don't feel obligated to teach the masses; when going back home to the Dominican Republic as an American, you will be called gringa because to them, you're white; when living in the U.S. as a Dominican-American, you will be called anything but white; when abroad, you're admired; when asked where home is? You don't know which one to choose because you have multiple dwellings; keep your mouth shut, don't be a snitch; bring your pilón, greka, and sofrito for your kitchen in college; always clean your meat with lime and water; don't be afraid to say that a green plantain is called plátano at home; be cautious of fixating on happiness, it comes from within; the American Dream is not your responsibility; understand that others already have what you're working towards; understand that means you have to put in more effort than the person next to you, but it will pay off; carry your culture with pride; speaking Spanglish counts as nothing; knowing two languages can get confusing for anyone;

the things that can get lost in translation are not just linguistic, they can be conceptual—values, education, memories, or even identity; embark on a new journey, but don't forget where you come from; always ask your parents for a blessing when you greet them, even in front of strangers, say bendición Mami o Papi; putting yourself first comes at a price, be ready to pay it; home is in the heart, it may shift forms from time to time, but it's always in your heart; just because something is new doesn't mean it's not meant for you; your journey will most likely be the first of many, so learn to trust yourself; don't dismiss your culture, celebrate it; let your accent be your way of speaking in cursive; navigating this world is hard, so find someone you trust or someone with experience to check in with frequently; make self-awareness a priority; true passion derives from pain; you are not a failure for not accomplishing your parents' goals; you are not a winner for achieving your parents' goals; trust yourself because, most times, you're all you will have.

Wife

By Suzanne Farrell Smith

At last, the mother of the birthday boy appeared in the backyard, struggling to carry an oversized cutting board piled with salami, cheese, olives, and crackers. Her crying toddler followed close behind. A cold front had swept into town, sending some of the arriving children inside. I kept mine out—virus mitigation died hard—despite the fact that I left their hats in the car. The mother wore a deep-cut navy blouse and no jacket. She looked lovely—amber hair blown out, makeup, earrings even, all of which seemed so *much* right as the pandemic began to ebb. Her arms strained and her heels strained too and I stared at those heels. How long had it been since I'd worn any footwear besides sneakers or snow boots? I'd been picking my children up from school in slippers.

The birthday mother arrived at the picnic table only one cracker short. Her toddler son clawed her leg, her preschooler daughter appeared from under the table and urgently repeated *Mommy*, and her eldest, the birthday boy, threw a toy out his second-floor bedroom window. Her smile didn't let up, but I recognized the way she breathed—a little tight. She gingerly stepped down a stone staircase, crossed to the woodpile, and loaded her arms with split logs for the fire pit. "Sorry I can't chat!" she said to us. I exchanged the kind of small talk with a few mothers that used to feel banal but now felt like a charge, like a renewed skill, like life was being lived again. *It's chilly, isn't it?* We all zipped up against the wind and volunteered to distribute juice boxes and red wine while the birthday mother collected gifts my children and others had left here and there in the yard.

More guests arrived, some fathers even. I always notice when fathers come to the birthday parties. It doesn't happen often. My father died young. My mother, a penny-pinching former teacher, was determined to throw birthday parties for my sisters and me. She wrote invitations by hand and baked cakes in the shape of trains or carousels. She'd erect a folding table in the garage—the only space large enough to hold everyone—and spread out hand-sewn cloth, then lead us and our friends through crafts. I don't recall these parties—they slipped, along with my father, into the space of loss—but I have plenty of photos that show us in paisley dresses and matching fabric party hats, at work on some ornament or paper heart.

After snacks and drinks, swings and ride-ons and chase, the birthday boy's father appeared. He greeted the other fathers with a robustness born, I suppose, of a pandemic's long-time-no-see. He made the same small talk, weather and whatnot, but somehow grew it big, so big that my companions and I could no longer hear each other. "Magnificent!" the birthday father exclaimed to one man about his hair, which was thick and carefully arranged, then pulled off his baseball cap and pointed to his naked scalp. He replaced the cap, grabbed a wine, and sat in a camping chair by the fire. The mothers and I ate manchego cubes and *mm-hmmed* to each other about how good it felt to be out.

When it was that time, the time you feel at every party when the ratio of fun to done starts to slide, the birthday father collected the Spiderman cake from the kitchen, carried it on another oversized cutting board, waited for us mothers to clear the picnic table, then set it in the middle. Children appeared, eyes bright, cheeks splashed. *Can I have that piece? I like chocolate. My favorite frosting is red. I want a corner!* I reminded my sons to ask with a please, though the father didn't seem to register their politeness. He looked around for something and, not seeing it, frowned. My instinct—or my training—is to help, so I leaned over the children's heads to ask what he needed. He ignored me, turned toward the house, and let out one word, taut and loud.

43

"Wife!"

I froze. He growled again.

"Wife!"

I looked around, but no one else seemed to take notice of the tone and the man who'd just discharged it.

I felt uncomfortable, instantly, maybe irrationally. I tried to peel him apart, grant him some grace. Was he afraid? Afraid of the children pushing into the cake, afraid of their raw spoken want? Afraid of being in charge of a thing that he was ill-equipped to manage, in charge of a thing at all? Perhaps he was out of social practice—we all were. Or it could be their marital thing, the words they called to each other no matter who was around. *Husband! Wife!*

But he didn't seem afraid or awkward or tender. Jaw tight, eyebrows bisected by a deep wrinkle, he seemed angry. Angry that, in all her prepping and coordinating, the birthday mother hadn't anticipated this moment, had missed one step in her party-planning list, had created the tenuous scenario in which he found himself, had abandoned him. And the only word he could muster in this charged state was that which he most needed and that which had let him down: *Wife.*

I remember this from a college sociology course: masculinity isn't something one has, it's something one does. Masculinity responds to and relates to others. And it shifts—dramatically—by place, by culture, by era. It's masculinity that came to mind as I observed the birthday father scowling. The kind prescribed in my mother's bible and reenforced by her conservative upbringing, the kind that kept her tethered to my father for her lifetime after he died, the kind that said she was always "and wife."

The etymology of "wife" is linked to the etymology of "woman." The difference is that "woman" attempts to name an adult human, while "wife" points to a relationship. One proposed root of "wife" listed in the Oxford English Dictionary is the Indo-European word "weibōn," which may have meant "to vacillate, fluctuate, move hither and thither" about the home. "Wife" as an active role. A function. Man performs masculinity, wife performs wifeness. Wife as crudité carrier, fire starter, gift collector. Wife as the person who, long after her husband dies, continues to move hither and thither, to throw the birthday parties, and never again looks for love.

The birthday mother, still in heels, still smiling, emerged from the house. She was carrying a cake knife the safety-prescribed way—fingers around the handle, forefinger stretched along the spine, tip down, cutting edge to the back. She placed the handle in her husband's palm so that the knife never touched the table around which the children were gathered. I couldn't help but believe this was, in fact, a deliberate step in her planning. Keep the knife in the kitchen until the last minute. Don't leave it on the table, not when the children will come close at the first sign of cake.

Everybody sang. The birthday father sliced. The birthday mother distributed. I stepped back into a role I'm not used to—passive observer. It occurred to me that no one had asked for my help.

On our wedding day, my husband and I chose a number of non-traditional elements. We'd gotten married ahead of time, in Manhattan's City Hall, so we could write our own ceremony and have a friend officiate. I did my own hair and refused to wear white. We served cupcakes. But much was traditional—chairs in neat rows overlooking Long Island Sound, live accordion music, the theater of it all. When it came time to be declared, we chose "husband and wife," only a slight change from my mother's "man and wife."

I don't mind inhabiting "wife." In my marriage, "wife" and "husband" aren't roles we perform so much as two halves of a pact. Wife, to me, says we're in this—this house, these children, these bills—together. We both move hither and thither. But the birthday father cheapened the word. Later, when I told my husband about it, he cringed. I told him I didn't know why it bothered me so much. "Because it's gross," he said. "He treated her worse than a dog."

How had no one else seen the man treat his wife worse than a dog?

But something I've come to understand about myself: I'm afraid of loud, angry men. For two decades, my husband has worked as a true-crime journalist covering scores of loud angry men who kill women—whose masculinity kills women. I grew up without a father or brother. My early male figures were elementary school teachers and Catholic priests. I've never been comfortable interacting with loud men. So maybe I misread this loud man. Conveyed it wrong to my husband, slanted the story to match my apprehension at what I perceived to be the man's dominance over his wife. Maybe he was angry and it was okay to be angry. Or maybe he wasn't angry at all. Just a loud man saying a loud thing over the loud voices of cake-hungry children. Whatever fuel ignited in him, I knew this for sure: I would not want to be his wife.

Post-cake, we moved inside for piñata time. The father strung the piñata from a beam while the children lined up behind the birthday boy for a chance to bat. But the boy shattered the papier-mâché lion with one blow. Candy skittered everywhere. One of my sons told me he was disappointed he didn't get to try, so I asked the father if he could restring the piñata.

"Just hold it for him," he said, handing me the wrecked thing. He gave my son the bat and I held the piñata as far as I could from my body. *Whack.* I couldn't keep my grip against the force, and the piñata fell for a second time.

"The *one* thing you were supposed to do!" said the birthday father to me, chuckling. The one thing. A missed step.

I gathered my boys and made sure they said goodbye and thank you to the birthday family. The mother and father stood together, her hand on his back, as the birthday boy ate candy, the preschooler bounced on the couch, and the toddler was nowhere to be found.

Cold from the long afternoon, we packed into the car. My sons told me they had fun at the party, mostly with each other. They told me that the cake was yummy, that the slide was fast, that the birthday boy played too rough. That even though it was chilly, it felt good to go to a birthday party again.

Between them on the back seat sat the piñata. "Take it," the father had said. "Now it's just garbage."

In Memoriam: A Triptych

By Elizabeth Hilts

I.

She called to ask how to tell if lamb was still good.
"I usually go by smell; does it smell okay?"
She couldn't tell, so I drove over.
"It's supposed to be a treat for A," she told me. "I was going to make
cassoulet while he's, you know, at the place where he goes." Recipes
her husband loved she could remember, but where he had worked
for decades eluded her.
There was no need to unwrap the butcher paper, but she insisted,
leaning in for a whiff of the ammoniated stench. "And see how
sticky it is? That's another way to tell," I said. How could A have
not noticed when he sat down to the breakfast she'd surely served
him before he went to teach at the university? The sausages had
gone off, too. I shoved all of it into a freezer bag, put that in three
plastic grocery bags, washed the refrigerator with white vinegar.
"I knew you'd know what to do," she said.
I drove to the dump with my car windows open.
She had taught me how to cook, taking me through the steps of
hand-made pesto and pasta, roast chickens stuffed with lemons
and garlic, fruit-jeweled tarts. A took over all the cooking once
Alzheimer's stole her knowledge of the hows and whens of it. He
told me that chopping onions was a kind of blessing.

II.

It was L's birthday and everyone was to bring something—bushels of
fresh clams, potato salads, platters of cured meats and grilled veggies,

and beautiful cheeses. She wanted my spareribs. I made eight racks, each step a process that takes time and care.

- Peel away the silver skin that clings to the back of the bones.
- The sharp grittiness of brown sugar against my fingertips still a surprise as I rub the spice blend into the meat.
- Wrap each rack in heavy aluminum foil to trap the flavors and make moist heat.
- Stack the bundles on sheet pans and bake slow for a few hours, shifting the bundles occasionally to make sure they all cook evenly.
- Pack them all in a cooler to be finished off at M's little cottage by the water.

L's dad fretted over his grandsons climbing on the seawall, paced back and forth between the two boys, reaching to steady them. "Goddammit," he shouted, though there was no danger; startled, the younger boy almost tumbled from his perch. The kids' father talked them into playing on the stretch of lawn just until their grandfather calmed down a little. The boys' mother soothed her dad and got him to sit down to eat.

"I like this," L's dad told me, holding up a rib. "What is it called again?" M's father kept asking for more, ate half a rack all by himself. Six of his eight children were there, and they gathered around watching him nibble and gnaw as if they'd never seen anything like it.

At the funeral for M's dad, less than a month later, M wrapped me in a hug, whispered, "He'd pretty much stopped eating. He'd forgotten how to enjoy food, until he had those ribs." By then L and her sisters had found a nursing home that specialized in the care of Alzheimer's patients. For years, they took turns bringing their father foods he loved, until he forgot how to swallow the things he chewed.

49

III.

There was going to be a big crowd for Thanksgiving that year, and I was in charge of pies. Requests for apple and pumpkin, of course. Pecan. Mincemeat, because there's one in every crowd. We were standing in B's kitchen the Saturday before when B told me her mother wanted some special kind of pie, but they couldn't figure it out, "and it's driving us both nuts." I watched as she began to help her mother J peel off the extra layers of clothing J had spent the morning pulling on. A pair of jeans, a red bikini bottom, corduroy pants. How did she have the patience?

"Can you give me a hint, J?"

J's fingers danced a circle. She licked her lips. "Yellow."

Almost as quickly as I conjured the flavors of yellow, B let me know I was wrong.

"Not Boston cream. Not coconut custard," she said.

"Nope, nope," J agreed.

"Not lemon meringue, either."

"Banana cream?" I asked as B got down to the final layer, a pair of wide-legged velveteen pants the color of garnets.

"Yes!" J rose from her seat. "Yes! Banana cream pie!" She clapped.

I clapped.

B clapped.

B's four-year-old daughter clapped and turned the words into a song that she started dancing to: "banana! cream pie! ba-na-a-a-ana! cre-e-em pie-ie-ie!"

J danced, too, and so did B, and so did I.

We clapped and sang and danced the small victory of joy.

Chasing Chickens in Connecticut: A Moment of Destiny Takes Our Writer Unawares

By Gina Barreca

I was making tomato sauce the other afternoon just as my Sicilian grandmother taught me: searing the sausage and the chopped meat in separate frying pans while getting the olive oil, garlic, parsley, and oregano ready in other small pots. In Brooklyn, where I grew up, we always had sauce—or what my family called "gravy"—simmering on a back burner. The ur-version had been there since 1945, maybe '46. Stirred constantly by my Aunt Josephina, who had an arm like a longshoreman, the only time the gravy was left unattended was when Josephine left her spot to go to Mass.

The women in my family used no recipes. They used small handfuls of salt, fistfuls of fresh basil, and spoons of olive oil. They were procured, drug-like, from somebody who had a connection to the good stuff. We didn't have a measuring cup. "You need a cup of something? There's one in the sink." That's how we learned to cook. The only way I can teach somebody how to replicate a dish is by having them watch me. In language, I can't explain it.

For Italians, cooking is more choreography than culinary.

My Sicilian family had the traditional kitchen arrangement in our family's Brooklyn, New York home: the upstairs kitchen was immaculate, perfectly equipped and too good to be used to cook a meal for anyone we actually knew. No meal was prepared in that kitchen. The only ones allowed to eat there would have been the people who could have sat in the living room that nobody ever used. That room had three pieces of matching brocade furniture covered in industrial grade vinyl, and the lampshades were still in the original cellophane wrapping. I once asked my grandmother if it was safe to keep cellophane so close to a light bulb. She grabbed me by the ear. "You turned the light on in the good living room?" I realized we were in no danger from anything incendiary: nobody would dare switch on a light.

The real meals, served on Sunday after church for the immediate family of 219, were prepared in a downstairs kitchen. As a kid, I promised myself that when I had my own house, I would never have a kitchen I didn't use. Plus, not for nothing, I promised myself that everything in my life would be different, too. So, now, picture me forty-five years later in my Connecticut kitchen, which is as different from the basement kitchen as it is possible: It's airy, big, and filled with windows that look directly into our tree-filled, stone-walled, two-acre backyard. Yet echoes of my childhood linger: the hiss of the meat, the garlic on the chopping board, the scent of basil on my fingers before I drop it in the pot. On this summer afternoon I'm cooking because we have a dozen friends coming over for dinner.

It's quiet enough to hear the bird sing and the meat sizzle, and I'm happy.

My husband, not Italian but from New Jersey—so it's almost the same thing—has gone to buy wine to accompany the meal.

Then I see the approach of the chickens.

We have new neighbors who live down a slight hill. It's clear their chickens decided, like characters out of an old war movie, to make a break for it. A dozen of them scramble over the stonewall and invade our yard. They're eating birdseed under the feeder like they've discovered the bounties of their own nation, and they are scratching up the mulch like they're looking for a fight.

A fight is what they're going to get. Within my bones, ancient strands of DNA awaken. There's no plan involved, no decision; I simply act. I run outside, slamming the screen door behind me, and scream in my already loud voice, a voice that sounds like gravel in a blender when I am at my most lyrical: "Get outta of my yard, you lousy birds!"

I chase them around the yard while flapping my apron as if brandishing a weapon. The graying bun at the top of my head is coming loose, with strands of curly hair covering my face. I look like a caricature of peasant life. Think Bruegel meets Scorsese.

Here's what you need to understand: everything I'd ever done in my life I'd done precisely to avoid this moment.

I stayed in school so long that I got my PhD. I wrote a bunch of books. I lectured around the world about how women everywhere need to unchain ourselves from traditional, cultural stereotypes that kept us from achieving true independence. A woman's right to invent new patterns and create new narratives, ones we could not yet even imagine had been, for years, my life's mission. It was, for god's sake, on my website.

And yet here I am on a hot July afternoon running after livestock while flapping my apron and cursing.

I am, in other words, doing exactly what my great-great-great grandmothers in Castelbuono, Sicily did to protect their hovel from the neighbor's goats. The only part that's changed? I'm swearing in English. I'm probably carrying the same heavy wooden spoon over my head, which is the universal gesture used by women under 5'2" to exaggerate our sense of threat.

I didn't realize that my husband had returned home and was witnessing this scene. When I saw him standing on the deck, I made a futile attempt to collect myself by tucking some stray hair back into the bun. In a cheerful, slow voice containing a small tinge of horror, he asked, "And, Gina, exactly what are you doing?"

I replied, "I'm becoming the woman I'm meant to be. It's destiny."

Michael did not look reassured.

We ate well that night. We did not have poultry.

An Invasion, a Witness, an Ambush

By Bessy Reyna

An Invasion: Panama City, December 20, 1989

Only four days before Christmas—when the city was in a festive mood and the street decorations glowed like gems competing with the stars in the tropical sky—the people in Panama City were awakened by the sounds of war planes from the United States. Members of the 82nd Airborne Division parachuted like jellyfish and thousands of soldiers took over the streets. That was the beginning of the invasion; ironically labeled by President George H. W. Bush as "Operation Just Cause."

Thirty-three years later, the exact number of civilians killed during that invasion is still unknown. Although an estimated 20,000 U.S. troops were in control of the city, they did nothing to stop the massive looting of grocery stores and other businesses. They also did nothing to help the hundreds of families left homeless after the bombs had demolished their homes and apartment buildings. The invading army did nothing to stop the chaos.

As a writer who grew up in Panama, where my family still lives, I felt compelled to record some of what had happened during the years of the dictatorships leading up to the invasion. To accomplish this, I submitted an application for an artist's grant, to the then CT Commission on the Arts, outlining the project which I titled "From Panama: The Voices You Never Heard." I was fortunate enough to receive their grant and by September 1990, I had saved enough vacation days and obtained a leave allowing me to travel to Panama.

Prior to my arrival I had booked a room at the Hotel El Ejecutivo. I needed a space that would provide me with the privacy required to conduct interviews with former political prisoners, exiles, and witnesses to the U.S. invasion. At the hotel I also had the space to work on the transcriptions and translations immediately. A friend had set up several appointments for me ahead of time. It was nine months after the invasion and people's lives were beginning to get back to normal. Many of the returning exiles were reclaiming their lives and had full-time jobs. For others, their jobs schedules made it difficult to meet during the day. I had to rely on childhood friends and people they knew who were willing to meet with me, either at the hotel, their homes, or offices.

Until 1968, Panama had been a democracy, but a number of military officers, supported by the U.S., decided to claim the country for themselves. The first era of the dictatorships started with Coronel Boris Martinez (1968-1969). Then came General Omar Torrijos (1969-1981) who was killed in a helicopter crash. The next one, Coronel Florencio Flores who lasted eight months (July 1981 to March 1982) and was deposed and ousted by Coronel Ruben Dario Paredes (March 1982 to August 1983). Paredes capitulated and passed on the reins, after having made a deal with General Manuel Antonio Noriega, whose drug-trafficking was the alleged excuse for the U.S. invasion. One after another, these brutal and corrupt men controlled the lives of the citizens of Panama for twenty-one years.

A Witness: Mariela Ledezma

"I will never forget the invasion for as long as I live," Mariela Ledezma told me, closing her eyes and covering her face. Ledezma was very attractive and wore an orange linen dress, matching purse, and shoes. Her hair was pulled back, freeing her face, so I could see all the emotions she was going through as we spoke. At the time of our interview, she was a law school student at the University of Panama. Ledezma and I had never met before and our meeting had been arranged by a mutual friend.

As soon as she arrived in the hotel room, she sat on the chair in front of me, took her shoes off, and lit a cigarette. Ledezma was charming—the type of person who makes you feel very comfortable right away. She was also intense and passionate about her love for the country, and very angry about the invasion and its aftermath. "I condemn the invasion, condemn it completely," she said.

"I was staying with my friend Lupe. We had been out during the night, admiring the Christmas decorations and drove to get ice cream. By then, it was so late that I decided to stay at her apartment instead of driving all the way back to mine. I had fallen asleep. In the early morning, Lupe shook me and shouted that we were being bombed." Lupe's apartment building was very close to La Comandancia, Noriega's military headquarters, one of the main targets.

Ledezma's cigarette shook in her hands. She was quiet for a while as her mind went back to that morning full of explosions. When she was ready, she began to describe how she and Lupe decided to protect themselves: "Because of the Rambo and war movies we'd seen, we decided to hide inside a walk-in closet." After a while they crawled under the dining room table since that was the only thing they could think of doing to protect themselves. The telephone rang and startled them. A friend called to tell them what was happening and to make sure they were safe. In the middle of the conversation, the phone went dead.

Lupe's dog wouldn't stop barking, and then she crawled out to get her small radio. They were shocked by the news and had no idea of the magnitude of what was happening. After a while Lupe decided to crawl over to look out the window. She saw a U.S. army tank parked between the apartment building and Noriega's headquarters. The Panamanian soldiers, supporters of Noriega, were firing back in the direction of the tank. Ledesma crawled to join Lupe by the window.

Inside the apartment she and Lupe didn't know what to do or what to expect. They waited for hours until they no longer heard gunshots. By then, the silence encouraged them to try to get out of the building and open the front door. That's when they came face to face with a U.S. soldier. The women attempted to talk to him, but he started shouting orders in English right away: "Get back in and close the door!"

Ledezma answered him in Spanish. The soldier told them that he was Puerto Rican and spoke to them in Spanish. He described some of the battles taking place around the city. "No one can leave this building," he said. The women began to cry. Seeing this, the soldier softened his tone as if understanding their distress. "Look, things are pretty bad out there right now. If you get out, you might get killed." While some areas of the city were not affected, Ledezma mentioned that: "It was not the same to have lived through the invasion in another area of the city that was not under attack, as to have been in the middle of it—in the worst possible area."

Some neighbors met on the staircase inside the building, and while some supported the invasion, others didn't. Ledezma was finally able to phone her family to let them know that she was safe. Two days later, a friend was able to reach Lupe's building and she, Lupe, and her dog were able to leave in his car. They drove to Ledezma's building and found it full of bullet holes.

"I was ten years old when the dictatorship started," Ledezma said. While in high school she used to shout: "Down with the military!" But she questions the rationale behind the invasion. The United States did not have to destroy the country's economy to get rid of Noriega. She recalls the chaos and looting following the invasion. "I get goose bumps telling you about this because you had to experience what happened that day. I can't forget how frightened I was. The images I saw. I can't forget them."

An Ambush

Before my trip to Panama City in September 1990, I'd heard rumors that gangs were attacking travelers on the road from the international airport to the city. The night of my arrival, my brother Ruben waited for me at the airport. We had not seen each other for several months, and on the road our talk centered on our elderly parents' health and his children. We both wondered about the country's future now that the dictators had been expelled by the U.S. invasion in December 1989.

We were traveling towards the city late at night and reached an area where the road narrowed. It was dark and very desolate. Even though there were no other cars in the area, Ruben stopped at a red light. Suddenly, we were surrounded by about six men in dark clothes. They quickly covered our windshield with soap. One of them banged on my window and another tried to open the door. Two others blocked the front of the car hitting the hood. My brother quickly turned on the windshield wipers and sprayed washer fluid to clear the view while yelling back at them. I was strangely calm and quiet. My mind raced searching for the numerous possible outcomes this encounter could have for us.

From the moment we were ambushed, I trusted that my brother would know what to do. This was his country. I, on the other hand, had become almost a foreigner. The city I left behind some twenty years before was now transformed to look like a mini-Miami or New York, full of skyscrapers that had replaced old and beautiful Spanish-styled homes. I kept wishing that the light would change or that the men would vanish. Instead, they kept banging on the car, hitting the hood, all while trying to force open the windows and doors.

Ruben and I had not said a word to each other during this attack, but when I looked at him, I noticed that he had slowly reached for something under his seat. When he raised his arm, I saw a Colt .45. Maybe I should have been afraid, but I wasn't. I was more worried about the possibility of a shoot-out happening at any moment than anything else.

The man by my brother's door looked at the gun, crossed his arms and yelled at my brother in Spanish: "You going to shoot me? Come on, shoot!" Then, just as suddenly as they had surrounded us, they disappeared into the dark bushes on the side of the road.

I had been on a road in Panama City for less than an hour, and I had already experienced the violence that had become part of daily life. When the light finally changed after what felt like an eternity, my brother floored the car. As my ragged breathing began to slow, I realized how very relieved I was that those thugs also didn't have guns. I didn't want to imagine what would have happened to us if they did, but the realization of how calm I had been during this whole experience was surprising to me. Here I was in a dangerous situation in which, luckily, one gun was enough to scare away these men. I found myself—an anti-gun person—having to accept the fact that it was one gun that made all the difference in this instance.

After a few minutes on the road, my brother looked at me, smiled, and in his typical fashion, joked: "I'm glad they went away. I was really enjoying our conversation." Later on, as I met other people in Panama, I learned that "joking" had become a way of surviving the uncertainties and dangers they had to confront on a daily basis during all those years living under the dictators' rules.

While driving around the city I noticed that there were private security guards with weapons in front of many of the businesses and in all of the banks. At a restaurant, a group of young musicians performed a song, and I have never forgotten the lyrics they sang: *"Por dentro, por fuera, de todos todos lados nos tiran balas. Nos tiran balas." From the inside, from the outside, from everywhere they are shooting at us. They are shooting at us.* And this was exactly how the people in Panama felt in those days. The bullets of the military were replaced by the bombs of the invasion, and now the attacks by assailants.

After my return to Connecticut, the difficult task of transcribing, translating and typing twenty interviews took a long time. It wasn't until I read each piece out loud that all of the emotions I had kept from surfacing burst out. My tears flowed for the inhumanity of the dictators, for the dead due to the invasion, and for the destruction of the country I loved. How long does it take for a country to heal the wounds inflicted by a dictatorship lasting over twenty years? How long will it take for people to forget how they had to survive without knowing the whereabouts of their loved ones? I wish I knew the answer.

Fiction

Trust Fall

By Chris Belden

We were out in the back yard, Richie and I, playing badminton. The boundaries were a couple of trees, a stone walkway, and the edge of the brick patio. I was twelve and my brother fifteen. I don't know why I was playing with him, given how competitive he could be, how ruthless and cruel. I'd wanted to go to the library, but he badgered me until I gave in. He called me a bookworm and said I was afraid he'd kick my ass. All true. He always won, and not once did he take it easy on me. If I was stuck way over on one side of the court, he would line drive the shuttlecock into the grass at the other end, raise his arms, and crow like Jimmy Connors at the U.S. Open. When I won the occasional point, he'd curse and swing his racquet at an imaginary version of his little brother—*swish swish swish*, and I was dead. Once, after I'd struggled to win three points in a row, he launched his racquet at a tree and cracked it in half. Good thing the badminton set came with four racquets because he broke another one by pounding it on the ground after I'd tied him at 15. He beat me 21-15 that day after digging out the one remaining racquet from the closet.

Today I was down 16-1, and Richie beamed with his typical combination of glee, superiority, and contempt. This being September, the sun had already made its rapid early-evening slide behind the house. Inside, our parents sat in the kitchen with their after-dinner drinks, and I could easily imagine them snorting, between sips, at their older boy's triumphant outbursts:

"Yes!"

"*That's* what I'm talkin' about!"

"You *suck*!"

Richie had won ten volleys in a row. But this time, after he served, I lunged and barely popped the birdie back over the net, and it landed in-bounds. 2-16.

"You got *lucky!*"

My serve. I was pretty good at it, when I got the chance. I rarely hit the net or served out of bounds. Richie stood near the net, ready to slam the birdie back at me, possibly directly at my face—one of his favorite strategies. It's hard to return a shot aimed between your eyes.

I hit a pop-up over Richie's head, and he had to hustle. He got to it and connected, but the birdie wobbled out of bounds. 3-16.

"*Crap!*"

The yard was now completely in shadow, and the air had turned chilly. The light in the kitchen window shone yellow and warm, and I wished I was in there with my parents, or better still, at the library.

"Hurry up, nitwit," Richie said.

I served to the exact same spot, which he wasn't expecting. He got there and eked the birdie over the net, but I was ready and slammed it at his feet before he could react. 4-16.

"*Piss!*"

I won three more points before Richie scored with a line drive aimed at my crotch. He laughed when I flailed and knocked the birdie out of bounds. 17-7.

"That's why it's called a shuttle*cock*," he said, pleased with himself, before winding up and serving directly into the net. 8-17.

I won the next four in a row. The curses flowed. Richie finally scored when I slipped and whiffed at another line drive. 18-12.

I could sense him growing more and more frustrated, which was my brother's main weakness. I could only beat him at something— poker, ping pong, HORSE—if he got angry at himself. It was as if the anger made him less coordinated, both physically and mentally. And lately, he'd been pissed off about a lot of things. School made him mad, our parents made him mad, his friends made him mad—and *I* certainly made him mad.

"You're going *down*, boy," he said, preparing to serve. He hit a high floater, and I set up to return it. The birdie seemed to take a full minute to come down, and as it fell, Richie screeched like a pterodactyl, trying to distract me. But I managed a clean rope of a shot to the far edge of the court, and he couldn't get there in time. 13-18.

He scooped up the shuttlecock and shot it at me like a bullet. When I walked back to serve, I smiled, knowing I now had a chance.

The day before, while horsing around in the yard, Richie had asked me to catch him in a trust fall, like we used to do when we were younger. One of us would stand in front of the other, facing away, and fall backward, trusting the other to catch him.

"Me first," he said.

We hadn't done trust falls in ages, and I wasn't sure how this would go—Richie now stood about six inches taller than me and twenty pounds heavier. He waited longer than I expected, trying to throw me off, which was what he used to do when we first played this game. "Come on," I said, and he finally fell back. Somehow I managed to grab hold under his arms before he could land on the ground, and with a grunt I pushed him back up to standing.

"Your turn," he said.

I stood in front of him and felt his presence right behind me. When we were younger, I would dread the backward fall—I was never sure if I could trust him to catch me—but Richie had always been there.

"Ready?" I said.

"Absolutely."

I shut my eyes and fell. I immediately knew he'd stepped away—I could sense him disappearing. My butt hit the ground first, then my elbows, and, finally, my head. It didn't hurt that much on the grass, though I scraped my elbow enough to draw a little blood. But I did experience a momentary sense of shock, the way I felt once when, in the dark, I'd misjudged a step and went sprawling. Richie laughed and laughed, and I ran inside so as to not cry in front of him.

I remembered this incident just before serving, and my anger seemed to have the opposite effect on me than it did on my brother. It traveled from my heart into my arm, giving me the strength to pound the shuttlecock far over Richie's head, but not too far as to be out of bounds. He didn't stand a chance. 14-18.

"You *dick*!"

I scored three more points: Richie returned one into the net, hit one out of bounds, and whiffed one. On my next serve, he barely returned it, but the birdie hit the top of the net and tumbled over. 19-18, Richie. He was just two points away from winning.

"Now," he said, grabbing the birdie off the ground and fixing me with a mad stare, "you *die*."

I couldn't believe I'd almost caught up. But if I lost the next point, I'd have to win the following two just to stay alive. (You must win by two points in badminton, a stupid rule.)

Richie backed up to the edge of the brick patio and stared at me for a moment. I had come to know that stare lately. It said, *Do not cross me*.

He held out the shuttlecock, dropped it, and swung. *Thunk*. He caught it at the edge of the racquet and the birdie wobbled out of bounds. 19-19, my serve.

Richie went to pound his racquet on the ground but thought better of it. Without saying a word, he picked up the birdie and whacked it toward me. He then positioned himself and waited for my serve.

"Come on, ya little *turd*," he said.

My heart felt too large as it pushed up against my ribs. I wished my parents would come out to the back porch—not so they could witness my potential victory, but so they could protect me if I managed to win.

65

My serve sailed over the net, Richie returned it easily, and we volleyed for what felt like an hour, back and forth, almost lazily at first, with no attempt to make each other run too far, and then Richie slapped one deep to my left. Somehow I reached it and popped it just over the net, and he barely managed to get under it and launch it high into the air before scrambling back to better handle my inevitable slam. I raised my racquet for the power shot, but when the birdie finally dropped, I barely tapped the thing so that it inched over the net and fell like a dead sparrow. 20-19.

"*Fuck*!" Richie cried. I waited for my father to show his face in the window, but he and my mother must have retired to the den to watch TV.

"You *suck*!" Richie added.

I didn't respond, didn't even grin, though I felt jubilant inside. And terrified. Should I lose the next three volleys on purpose? I was quite capable of doing so, and of making it look natural. But I wouldn't lose on purpose. I wanted to win.

Richie, jittery and jangly, waited for my serve.

I bulleted the birdie over the net, and Richie shot it straight back at me. He'd hit it so hard, all I had to do was hold out my racquet and the shuttlecock pinged back over. He returned it off to my left, and I backhanded it toward the opposite corner. Richie barely arrived in time to send the birdie down the line. For a second I thought I'd lost this point, but I stretched and managed to pop it over. Surprised, Richie was slow to move. He charged forward and dove, his racquet just able to scoop the birdie up and across. But now he lay flat on his belly. I knew I had him. I reached the shuttlecock easily and swatted it over him. We both watched it land a good two feet in-bounds.

21-19!

I looked down at Richie. He looked up at me. I glanced toward the house behind him. I'd never make it past him to the door. I had only seconds.

I ran.

Behind our house lived the Caserta family. I tore through the narrow opening that had been worn down by foot traffic between the hedges that separated our back yards. The Casertas' terrifying German Shephard, Otto, barked from a window as I zipped down a hill into the Conleys' yard next door. I followed a path alongside their house to their front yard and 22nd Street. Not sure which way to go, I hesitated before turning right, toward Logan Avenue. I didn't once look behind me, but I could hear my brother huffing back there and the slap of his Converse sneakers on the sidewalk. From the sound of it, he was about twenty yards behind.

At Logan Avenue, I turned left, heading toward the 25th Street branch of the public library. They were open until eight, but I didn't know what time it was now. I prayed the doors were not locked.

My brother was athletic, but I managed to stay ahead of him past 23rd and 24th Streets. Twenty-fifth was a busy thoroughfare, and I knew I might need to pause to let cars pass before crossing. If that happened, Richie would catch me for sure, so I resolved to turn right if necessary and head down to Market Avenue, a major road where there would be plenty of witnesses in case Richie caught up and started whaling on me.

Luckily, traffic was light, and I shot across 25th toward the library. I saw several cars in the parking lot and a couple of bikes where I would park my own when I visited. I yanked open the front door leading into the vestibule with its flyer-clotted bulletin boards and then entered the second door into the library proper. Not once had I looked back.

The library was one large room with the main desk in the middle. On three sides stood orderly rows of bookshelves where I'd lose myself and all track of time whenever I could. The place was blessedly quiet. All I could hear as I staggered toward the periodicals section near the front door was the frantic pounding of my heart. Miss Laura, the librarian, watched curiously as I sat and tried to catch my breath. She was a skinny older lady who always wore her hair in a bun and a cardigan sweater over her dress. I waved to her, attempting to be nonchalant despite my wheezing, then turned my attention to the door. I waited, one minute, then two, but Richie did not enter. I thought of vampires unable to pass the threshold of a church.

The clock read 7:47—thirteen minutes to closing. Would Richie wait outside for me, like a patient lion watching for an injured antelope to wander off from its herd? Able to breathe now, I walked over toward a window. There, by the bike rack, paced my brother, arms across his chest, gazing up at the sky. He looked mad—not in an angry way, but a crazy way, as if I'd stolen his wallet or his Who albums rather than beat him in a game of badminton. The sky was turning dark, and I wondered if our parents had noticed our absence. Probably not. They were likely waiting for *The Flip Wilson Show* to start.

"Attention, attention," Miss Laura announced over the PA system. "The library will be closing in ten minutes. If you need to check out books, please come to the front desk now. Thank you."

As several people lined up to check out their books, I wandered over to the cinema section and read about Stanley Kubrick for ten minutes. I'd recently watched *Paths of Glory* on TV. Apparently, while directing *2001: A Space Odyssey*, Kubrick wore the same style of clothes every day so as not to bother with yet another decision.

When the fluorescent lights flickered, I joined Miss Laura at the door. She shut out the lights and removed the keys from her purse.

"Did you ride your bike, Carl?" she asked.

"No, I walked."

In the vestibule, she locked the inner door. I hoped that, at least for a moment, her presence would stop Richie from pouncing on me when we left the building. But when we pushed through the outer door, my brother was nowhere to be seen.

"It's getting dark," Miss Laura said.

The sky had turned a dark blue, and the clouds glowed pink with the light of the set sun. I hoped my parents were too engrossed in the TV to notice that the streetlights had turned on.

"Will you get home okay?" Miss Laura asked.

I wanted her to offer me a ride, but I couldn't bring myself to ask. "Oh, sure," I said. "It's only a few blocks."

"Well, all right then," she said, smiling. "G'night, Carl."

I watched her walk to her car at the far end of the otherwise empty parking lot. As she pulled away, I expected Richie to leap out from around the corner of the building, but nothing happened. I crossed 25th Street and headed up Logan Avenue, shivering from both the chilly night air and the dread of the inevitable attack. TV light flickered in living rooms, bats darted overhead. Every time I passed a tree I clenched myself in anticipation. I turned up 21st Street and, at our house, walked cautiously up the driveway to the side door. I saw no one.

Inside, I heard the TV from the far end of the house. I walked slowly through the dining room, the front entryway, the living room, still waiting to be pounced upon. In the den I found my parents and brother watching Flip Wilson dressed as Geraldine. My father laughed loudly, an infectious laugh that almost made me smile.

My mother glanced over and said, "Where've you been, sweetie?"

"The library," I told her, knowing she'd approve. She nodded and turned back to the TV.

Richie lay on the sofa. He laughed along with our dad and—very purposely, I felt—avoided looking at me. I considered joining them, but then I'd have to ask Richie to make room for me. He knew that it would be hard for me to ask, which was why he lay across the entire sofa.

I went upstairs and read *The Hobbit*, brushed my teeth, got into my pajamas, and climbed into bed. At nine o'clock, my mother tucked me in and switched off the light. I lay wide awake listening to her and my father turning the pages of their books. From next door I could hear the tinny thump of drums and bass from Richie's headphones. It seemed like I was now finally safe from my brother. Still, I couldn't sleep. Not because I felt afraid, but because I felt jazzed from the amazing sense of accomplishment: I had beaten Richie at badminton! It was like a movie in which the underdog claws his way from certain defeat to victory with a combination of athletic prowess and psychological strategy. That final, game-winning volley over Richie's prone body—I relived it over and over.

Then, just as I started to drift off, I felt a cold hand clutch my ankle. I shrieked, my heart almost stopping cold. Richie had slowly, stealthily crept along the floor into my room, leaving the music playing in his room as a decoy, and reached under the blankets to grab me. I sat up, and in the deep, black quiet that followed, heard a cruel giggle recede in the darkness toward the open door.

Bittersweet

By Michael Belanger

Bittersweet curled around the skinny oak, tendrilled vines creeping toward the turquoise sky. In gloved hands, she worked methodically, cutting and pulling, pulling and cutting, until she had cleared a small part of the woods. The tree heaved a sigh of relief as she clipped the last of it, its trunk springing upright, no longer stooped, youth restored. Leaf meadow and underbrush spread around her, and as she wiped the sweat off her forehead, she took a deep breath, inhaling the sweet and earthy smell. Nearby, two fawns tiptoed on stilted hooves, reminding her of the stick figures Hazel used to draw, an oval atop four pencil-thin lines. She scanned the woods for their mother but couldn't find her. She gathered a pile of bittersweet in her arms, unable to escape the feeling of impending doom: a doe thrown to the side of a road, tongue lolling out of her mouth, tail fluttering from passing cars.

She carved a path through the woods, careful to avoid roots knuckling through the ground. Glancing at the sky, she traced a lattice of branches, as if a thatch roof sat atop this roughhewn forest: rugged yet refined. Her nose itched, and as she reached a hand over the pile of bittersweet, a spindly twig poked her in the face, as if mocking her progress. A small bush of raspberries, shrunken and deformed, cascaded into the trail, its thick stalks dotted with prickers. She glided along, popping a couple of wild raspberries in her mouth.

A train rumbled in the distance, and for a moment, she worried she'd see the colossus steaming through the forest, as if two paintings had been accidentally melded together. The train's horn hurried her along, and as she walked faster, listening to the crinkle of leaf and branch, she spotted another tree ensnared, strangled by bittersweet.

It was as if the branches had conspired against this poor oak, climbed up and down its body with murderous intent, a slow suffocation. She placed the pile down and reached for her gardening shears. She clipped the bittersweet around the trunk and added the vines to the stack. The oak wasn't free, but it would have to do.

Dark gray smoke billowed over the tree line, as if the train had suddenly taken off, chugging steadily through the air. She got the funniest feeling of living inside not one painting, but an entire museum: the pictures changing mood and tone and style, hands sketching and coloring from far away. For a brief moment, she even imagined one of Hazel's stick figure animals careening through the forest, escaped from a dusty bin in the basement. Walking faster now, she noticed more trees succumbing to the onslaught of the bittersweet: young trees with barely any leaves; old trees standing steadfast amidst the tumult, their bark scarred and bruised by the vines; spindly looking wisps bent-backed and sickly. Arms already full, she made a pact to return tomorrow.

Prometheus's Fire

By Rowan Marci

Dr. Thea Dumont sat at their white desk in their white office across from aerospace technician Leander Kostas, Applicant 04327.

Kostas wouldn't meet their gaze. But Dumont knew he was the kind of man who preferred this illusory face-to-face meeting over messaging or simulated voice chat. He still felt it was more "personal." So Dumont had added decorative touches to their virtual office: nickel detailing on the white leather armchair Kostas bobbed his leg in, framed floral prints for his darting gaze to land on.

"What did you want to see me about, Leander?" they asked.

"It's—it's happening again, Doc." Kostas ran a hand through his wavy hair.

"What's happening, Leander?"

"The...the..." In lieu of an explanation, Kostas tapped an open palm against his breastbone. He blinked rapidly, though his avatar had no tear ducts with which to cry.

He didn't have to explain. He'd come to Dr. Dumont more than once with these vague complaints of dissatisfaction.

The doctor leaned back in their chair, studying him. They remained puzzled as to why the aerospace technician had chosen to retain his Earth-bound appearance when he could have picked any form for his avatar. Dumont had personally opted to blunt their silver-black hair and their body's feminine features, adopting neutral pronouns. What was the point of gender markers, they thought, when procreation was no longer necessary? But Kostas's avatar in the Helix looked just as he had on Earth, down to the laugh lines around his liquid brown eyes and the cochlear implant scar hidden behind his left ear.

Dumont folded their hands on the desk. "You've been taking up hobbies, haven't you? Like I suggested?"

Kostas nodded at his lap. "Golf. Chess. Water skiing. It's not the same..."

"You titrated the difficulty level to your preference?"

"It's not. The same." Kostas sighed and combed his long fingers through his hair again. "It's just...none of this feels *real*."

Dumont frowned. They'd expected user feedback on the Helix's virtual environment. They wanted it. The project was still in the test phase, after all: ten thousand beta users rather than the entirety of the ten-billion-strong human population. But Dumont had been modifying the program for nearly a decade, and in their estimation, the platform was ready. Maddeningly, Kostas still wasn't satisfied.

"If the virtual environment doesn't feel real enough, Leander, you can bump your sensory registration levels up another notch."

"It's not that." Kostas leaned forward. "Take golf, for example. Before, there would have never been a choice about how easy or difficult it would be to learn it."

"Of course there was a choice. The amount of effort we put in determined the speed at which we acquired skill. It's no different here." Dumont had been told, back on Earth, that their tone could be curt. In the Helix, they'd chosen a soothing parental voice mod for occasions such as this.

"No, there were other factors. *Physical* factors." Kostas gestured to his absent cochlear implant. "Because we had *bodies*."

Early on in the project's development, one of the lead engineers had suggested that Dumont had vastly underestimated how much stock people put in their identities. Dumont had envisioned the Helix as a society cleansed of race and culture. Without bodies, things like age, gender, and sexual preference would become a moot point. There would be no need to fight over physical resources. Theological debates would become redundant, since mankind would transcend the need for a god. Everyone would belong to a collective consciousness without language barriers, social or class divisions. It would be a symbiosis of coexistence, a utopia of intellectual freedom.

But apparently, that vision was too idealistic. People didn't know how to let go of the past, even if the past was harming them.

"If it makes you more comfortable, Leander, you can turn off your auditory input." Maybe that engineer had been right, and Kostas was nostalgic for his Earth-bound identity. "We can all download sign language–"

Kostas cut them off. "That's not what I meant. What I'm saying is, there were always things we couldn't control, before. We got injured. We got tired. We got sick. Hell, we got old and *died.*"

All things that limited them. All factors Dumont had made obsolete. In the Helix, humankind could exist in its purest form: thought, the essence of what made them them. Dumont and their team had worked tirelessly to develop a program that could map human psyches, even down to the patterns of physiological response that produced emotion when (to the doctor's surprise) it became clear that users still wanted to experience them. The Earth may have been doomed, but Dumont had found a path to liberation. Just like the Greek god Prometheus, whose gift of fire launched mankind into an age of enlightenment, Dumont had granted humanity this gift of freedom.

Only Kostas didn't seem to be grateful.

Dumont stifled a sigh. "Have you tried meeting someone, like we talked about?"

When Kostas applied to the Helix project, his wife and daughter had already succumbed to the unstable, radiation-plagued conditions on Earth. But these days, who hadn't lost someone? Dumont had been twelve when they'd watched workers load their parents' bodies into the incinerator. Some days, the grief had come on so strong it felt as though their body would rip apart from the inside. But that had been forty-one years ago, and in the Helix, Dumont's eyes remained dry.

75

"Meeting someone isn't going to solve the problem, Doc." Kostas didn't seem offended by the suggestion. He seemed disappointed. "I know you don't want to hear this. But I think…" He drew a deep breath, hesitance not quite dampening the resolve in his eyes. "I think this whole thing may have been a mistake."

Foul heat spread through Dumont's simulated gut. No one had ever dared to call the Helix a mistake in their presence. The word reverberated through the doctor's coded synapses, contaminating places far deeper than that of mere pride. The Helix was their reason for being. And Kostas's mournful eyes no longer looked so innocent.

Dumont stared at him. Then, slowly, they smiled.

"I have just the solution for you."

Dr. Thea Dumont circled their drone higher around the half-completed Helix II. Using the drone's optics, they watched construction bots scurry along the emerging blue-gray spiral and weld steel panels onto the supercomputer's frame. On the opposite side of Earth's orbit, the original Helix drifted. The massive server was a feat of engineering, revolutionary for its time, currently host to Dumont's consciousness and that of ten thousand test subjects. But it was just the beginning.

Millions of miles away, just outside Mercury's orbit, a solar energy harvester gathered a small share of the sun's massive megawatt output. The harvester, which Dumont had lovingly named Prometheus's Fire, transmitted its collected energy via infrared laser to power the Helix. Every day, more solar panels were launched from Mercury's surface, adding to the web that stretched across a mere fraction of the sun's circumference. In time, though, a swarm of the thin silvery kites would surround the sun by the quadrillions, reflecting solar rays into a network of stellar energy harvesters to power an untold number of man-made structures throughout the solar system. Structures like the Helix I and II, which would house the liberated consciousness of the entire human race.

This was Dumont's vision, the next phase of humankind's evolution. It was hard for the doctor to suppress a swell of pride as they watched the construction bots manifest their dream. Their thoughts drifted into memory: themself as a wiry pigtailed girl, taking first place at the science convention over a group of glowering teens. Mama and Papa, so proud. Months spent sick in bed, in and out of hospitals, their mobile computer their only friend. Late nights spent on doctoral coursework in their isolation chamber, fierce determination dogging every keystroke.

Dumont had known suffering. But it had all been worth it for this.

Like Prometheus, Dumont had granted mankind a freedom no one could have dreamed. And they'd be damned if they were going to let Kostas question it.

The decision to move him to ground operations on Mercury wasn't a banishment, per se. Kostas was a competent technician, more than capable of operating the bots that mined Mercury's ore and fabricated the hematite panels that were launched into the sun's orbit. Dumont had done him a kindness, really. The work was physical. Kostas had to download his consciousness into robotic strip miners, maintenance and repair bots in the refineries and fabrication plants. It would make him feel like he had a body again. That had been what he wanted, hadn't it?

In any case, the move seemed to be working. In the months since the transfer, Dumont hadn't heard any complaints from Kostas at all.

The doctor paused the drone to toggle their consciousness into the construction site's monitoring system. The doctor preferred to focus on this: the big things, the important things, not single dissatisfied users. Then an alert pinged into their comms.

SOLAR PANEL LAUNCH TUBE FAILURE, MERCURY ZONE C-5.

Dumont closed it. Equipment failures like this were part of day-to-day operations, something the technicians could handle. The doctor scanned the operational stats of the construction bots, half-waiting for a confirmation message from the Mercury ground crew. Lines of data streamed through Dumont's view pane, but no confirmation message arrived.

Mercury Zone C-5, they messaged. *What's your status?*

A crewman responded. *We can't seem to locate the source of the error. We ran all the equipment checks. It doesn't look like a mechanical failure.*

Dumont closed out of the Helix II's stats. If the problem wasn't mechanical, then it could be a glitch in the launch sequence programming. Something a competent technician should be able to catch.

They messaged Kostas directly. *Leander, can you look into this?*

There was a delay–a longer delay than there should have been. And when a response came, it was not from Kostas, but from the crewman who had messaged before.

Dr. Dumont, you might want to come. Kostas has gone dark.

It takes two hundred fifty-seven seconds for a wirelessly-transmitted signal to travel from Earth to Mercury. Just over four and a quarter minutes for Dumont's consciousness to complete the transfer. Plenty of time to run through all the possibilities.

When Kostas had applied for the project, Dumont thought he believed in the Helix. He'd passed the psychological evaluation with flying colors. He had no familial ties back on Earth to make him regret leaving his body behind.

There had been no reason for him not to adapt.

Two minutes and thirty-eight seconds of data transfer remaining.

Dumont was no tyrant. Just as on Earth, no one in the Helix, including network architects, could spy on another's thoughts. One was even permitted to hide their unique network location temporarily, "go dark" for a time.

So what was Kostas's goal? Had he succumbed to another bout of ennui, abandoned his ground crew in the middle of a work day?

Had he failed to correct the launch tube problem and gone dark out of shame? Or, as Dumont suspected, was the intent more nefarious?

Was he trying to sabotage the project's construction?

One minute and forty-four seconds of data transfer remaining.

Kostas had called the Helix a mistake. Dumont had assumed a little demotion would remind him of all he had to be grateful for. Instead, it seemed to have fueled his rebellion.

Fifty-seven seconds of data transfer remaining.

That sour sensation of dread had returned, but Dumont fought to quell it. Yes, users could go dark for a time. But they always left footprints.

Twenty-two seconds of data transfer remaining.

Before they'd left Earth's orbit, the doctor had put Mercury's network administrators on the task of locating Kostas. He could be traced based on his last known location, especially if he had taken a bot offline.

Dumont was going to find him.

Data transfer complete.

The doctor came to awareness within the rough utilitarian network of Mercury's operations system. Immediately, they pinged their admins.

Have you located Kostas yet?

A programmer named Hamadani responded. *He was last tagged in a mining bot in Zone D-8.*

And where is that bot now?

On full automation.

Dumont swallowed their growing disquiet. *Are any of the other bots offline? Any signs of tampering in the launch program sequence?*

There were some alterations to the code that may have caused the shut-down, Hamadani admitted. *We're working on that. But at the moment, all of the surface bots are still online.*

Dumont scanned the inventory to confirm that the admin was correct. All mining bots, refinery, fabrication plant and launch equipment were operational and accounted for. So where the hell was Kostas?

Continue the trace, the doctor commanded. *Alert me immediately if any equipment goes offline.*

Yes, Dr. Dumont.

For a few moments, the doctor combed through Kostas's user history. He'd opened fabrication plant D at 0558 hours. Ran equipment checks at 0611. Exchanged pleasantries with other operators at 0615, 0618, and 0621. Downloaded into a mining bot at 0632. Nothing out of the ordinary until he abruptly disappeared at 1047, two minutes before the launch tube failure in zone C-5.

Dumont hastened to enter their override code and force a message past Kostas's blocks. *Leander. It's Dr. Dumont. Where are you?*

Mercury's operations network hummed with its usual activity: the vibrant sparks of human lives, the predictable sequence of automated functions. But Dumont's comms stayed silent. No alerts. No flags for unusual activity. No messages.

Leander. Talk to me. After a moment, they added, *Whatever you're going through, I can help.*

Silence.

Frustrated, the doctor switched to C-5's launch tube sequence and watched the programmers correct the altered code. With growing panic, they downloaded into the mining bot Kostas had last used, scanning it for signs of sabotage.

Dr. Dumont. The alert pinged bright and red, and Dumont froze. It was Hamadani. *A flag just came up in Sector Two.*

The doctor ought to have left the mining bot straight away. They'd have found Kostas faster if they'd uploaded directly to a piece of equipment in Sector Two, the expanding solar field meant for a new solar generator. But that wasn't what Dumont did. Instead, they toggled to the mining bot's exterior cameras, unable to resist the urge to peer into the hazy sky. They wouldn't see much. But old habits seemed to die hard.

The strip mine was a jagged pit of gray-brown cuts and heavy tracked equipment dotting Mercury's surface. But the scene around them faded from view as the doctor scrolled the bot's cameras skyward. Against the sun's glare, the swarm of solar panels was barely visible, a grid of tiny gray pinpricks along the star's southeast quadrant. Up there was the energy harvester Dumont had named Prometheus's Fire...and, somewhere, Kostas.

If the Helix was the heart of this project, the power plant nestled among that distant solar array was its lifeblood. A prickle of protective fear ran along the doctor's simulated spine.

Leander, they messaged. *I'm coming.*

Dumont uploaded into the monitoring system of Prometheus's Fire. The transfer was faster than it would have been to the solar field, as they'd already spent so much time in the energy harvester. The doctor split their visual field, scanning Sector Two's bots in their left pane, orienting Prometheus's cameras toward the new solar array on the right. In their left pane, they located the administrative red flag: a fuel transport pod that had gone offline. On the right, Dumont peered through Prometheus's eye, searching the void of space.

Leander, you cannot hide.

They'd find him. And when they did, this madness would come to an end.

An oblong shape in the distance caught their attention. They zoomed Prometheus's cameras in. It was the missing fuel transport pod, represented as an inactive, blinking dot on Sector Two's monitoring system. The pod hovered miles away, unmoving, uncertain.

Dumont quickly entered their override code to compel the pod back online. The action was denied. They tried to force their way into the craft, but met only firewalls.

Desperation scorched their consciousness as they stared at the pod. It looked innocuous from this distance, suspended in orbit like the silver-gray betta fish the doctor used to keep in a bowl at their bedside. But the vehicle was not harmless. When fully loaded, each pod carried two hundred thousand pounds of liquid gas which created five million pounds of force when combusted.

Offline, the vehicle had limited functionality. No unique actions. Manual control only. But it could follow its charted course. It could accelerate. And it was aimed directly at Prometheus's Fire.

Dumont activated their simulated video chat. They watched their face, the one they'd designed for the Helix, pop up in their visual field. "Whatever you're thinking of doing, Leander, don't do it."

They didn't expect to see Kostas in return, his olive skin, his crooked nose. But it was a surprise to hear his low voice over the comms, the way he rounded his vowels when he spoke.

"It's time to let go, Doc," he said. "I know you're just trying to save us. But this isn't how people are meant to live."

"Leander—"

"It's okay, Doc." There was a hitch in Kostas's voice, as if he was crying. But to cry, one needed a body. "It's okay. Dying can be beautiful, too."

Dumont couldn't speak as the pod roared to life, spitting blue flame and lurching toward Prometheus's Fire. They couldn't speak, but they wanted to scream. They wanted to rage, tear at their hair, claw at their chest. As they imagined their life's work reduced to debris, chunks of steel and severed wire spinning off into space, they wanted to feel their fist sink into the soft flesh and pliant bones of Kostas's face. For the first time in decades, they longed for a body, however flawed that body may be. They wanted to feel this agony with their entire being.

But the pod never made it to Prometheus's Fire. Long before it came within range, a flare shot along the vehicle's oblong hull. It exploded, a shower of orange and gold illuminating the darkness like a newborn star.

Dumont's rage cooled to numbness as hydrogen mixed with oxygen, shredding the pod's aluminum frame into unrecognizable bits. Micro explosions followed, the vehicle's fuel lines and propulsion systems erupting, electronics sparking blue. Shreds of the pod whirled toward the sun, caught in its gravitational pull. Dumont watched, and slowly pulled up Kostas's user files in their left view pane.

Every user in the Helix was subject to mandatory backups. Dumont's team didn't want any of their people lost. But at 1107 hours that morning, Kostas had deleted his entire backup history. The only place he'd existed until a moment ago, as far as he knew, had been inside that fuel transport pod.

Realization sank in as the dying pod's flames faded to sunset red. Kostas had meant to delete himself. True, the transport pod had been aimed at Prometheus's Fire. But Kostas had never been the type to take ten thousand others down with him.

An old ache flared to life inside Dumont's chest. Simulated though it was, the engineers had done a stellar job recreating emotions, the same ones that had plagued the doctor on Earth. Regret. Grief.

They recalled that sensation of acute longing from moments before, the animalistic urge for embodiment. A corporeal desire for pain.

Dumont shut their sensory registers off.

Scrolling through their administrative files, they arrived at their private cache of user copies. They selected Kostas's latest backup, the one that had been duplicated and saved without his knowledge at 0945 hours that morning.

Applicant 04327, Leander C. Kostas. Cisgender male. Age 45.

Dumont hovered over the "restore" function. Kostas had been a promising applicant. Accomplished, knowledgeable. Worked well with others. It would be a shame to lose him. The project needed people like him.

And they could not allow the Helix to appear a failure.

Dumont racked their consciousness for a reason things had gone wrong. They'd have to make more tweaks to the program, bring in more experts to enhance the virtual environment.

But, in the end, Kostas hadn't wanted this. And perhaps Dumont would never understand.

They liked to think it was guilt they felt as they dragged Kostas's file into the folder labeled "Archives." Frustration would have been wrong. Resentment, even more so.

The doctor placed Kostas's last backup in the archives folder and closed it, turning Prometheus's cameras away from the shell of his transport pod, preparing their story for the rest of the administrative team.

They did not linger on the seven hundred and eighty-six other users in the archives folder, lined up by applicant number.

Lost

By M.K. Bailey

A hand, a leg, an eye, a lip, a cock. The parts of man I see at night. I came here to be alone and was alone—then, too alone. They keep coming and coming and I keep coming and it's too much but it's not enough and I can't tell the difference between them anymore. They save me and condemn me to life.

They feed me, wash me, bring me each day. I warm myself in their desire. I move through worlds and worlds—no life has ever been so fully lived as mine. I am lost.

And they are lost too but don't know it at first. They try to leave, just like I did. They make a big deal out of saying goodbye. They open the door, look back, wave, then disappear into the snowy woods. But sooner or later they return and pretend to be angry. They tell me they're trapped, that they can't find their way out. They blame this on me, accuse me of casting some sort of spell over them, but I haven't.

The woods have closed their doors.

Eventually they stay. The urge to leave dissipates and they are mine. They pile up in corners, drift in and out of the darkness to where I lie. Is it love or the mesmerizing quality of the landscape that keeps them here? When I found this spot in the woods, this abandoned cabin, I didn't want to leave either. But I tried. I walked for days, crying, always crying, hacking through the brush, trying to remember the way out. Out to the mini-mart with its buzzing purple light? Then what? To another job, another car, another man? So I came back and sat on the rock ledge where nothing can see me but I can see everything—the jagged mountains to the north, the river valley flowing west, and a spring-fed lake just a ten-minute walk due south. The lake sparkles blue like a giant sapphire cast down by the gods. Here, I could be happy. And for a moment, I was.

The first one knocked at the door. I was asleep, wrapped up in an old bear skin. It was winter by then. Winter came early. An endless night of snow and howling wind. It is still winter. Now they don't knock. They come in of their own accord, unbidden and lie down beside me without words and I welcome them. All of them. They bring me gifts, food that dissolves on my tongue like cotton candy, evening gowns made from recently-hatched butterflies, books that float above my head and flip their pages just when I want them to. Sometimes I flatter myself, imagine a line of men extending from my door across the valley.

But the first one knocked. I ignored him, thought it was a branch brushing against the roof. But the tapping persisted, then an enfeebled "Hello?" I almost didn't answer. After all, I'd finally found a comfortable position—curled up, hands between legs, forehead pressed against knees—and I didn't feel like sharing. After so much pointless movement, I'd decided not to move anymore. Movement creates problems, needs, desires. Movement incites more movement. But the knocking continued, louder and louder, until it was a pounding in my head: hello, hello, hello, is anyone there? Who else had lost themselves in this wilderness? Or maybe I had been found. Lost or found, same difference. Hello, are you there? Yes, I am. But was I? I had to know and suddenly I was standing and wearing a black dress. A candle burned on the mantle. How nice. I opened the door and the pounding stopped.

At first I saw nothing but blackness and snow. Cruel night. Then a fish floated forward, twirling, as if caught in an eddy of snow. I looked around and saw a hand above the fish, then an arm, then the drawn and purple face of a man. A fisherman. A greasy, hook-riddled hat sagged over desperate eyes. He was a skinny one, engulfed in waders, a rifle slung over his shoulder. But the fish was big and plump. Come in, fisherman.

I stepped back and he stepped in.

"Thank you," he said in a voice so quiet and hoarse I could barely hear. "It was the strangest thing."

I said nothing. I had nothing to say. I hadn't said anything in weeks.

Half frozen, he shuffled to the stove. "It's out," he said. I hadn't noticed, or else I'd made the necessary adjustments. He started a fire and I remembered the existence of tea so we drank some, and he told me his story. I had forgotten mine—good riddance. He was Mac from Dubuque, a family man on vacation from his wife and kids—a fisherman in search of salmon. He took off his hat and scratched his balding head. "It was the strangest thing," he said. "I couldn't find my car."

They don't like to admit they're lost. But eventually they settle down. Priorities change. New values emerge. Warmth. Skin. Small repeated motions.

Mac cleaned and cooked the fish. I lay back down on the bear skin. I'd done enough. So a man was cooking me a fish. Then what? His presence already annoyed me—his constant sniffle, the way he kept stumbling on the uneven floor, the rustle of his clothes. The dark, sickly odor of him forced me to take shallow breaths.

I looked at Mac's rifle leaning against the wall—such a sleek decisive thing. I could aim from the hip, a quick tug of the finger then no more man. He looked half-dead already. He wouldn't know what hit him. But the fish was done and you can't kill a man after he's cooked you dinner. How right and wrong I was to want to be alone. How quickly solitude gives way to multitude. Now desire buzzes around me like an angry fly and I am, once again, insatiable.

We sat on the floor and ate with our fingers. No one spoke except the fish. Its tender flakes melted on my tongue. Soon nothing was left but the eyes. What would they taste like? Slippery, salty balls swallowed whole. I ate them for perspective.

The fisherman unfolded a map and turned it in my direction. "Where are we?"

I shrugged my shoulders and smiled.

He stared at me. His eyes were the color of low clouds before rain. I watched his brow tense, his jaw clamp down. He was starting to look familiar.

"What's that supposed to mean? You don't know? How could you not know? You live here."

I continued to smile.

He groaned. Pounded his fist on the floor then swore under his breath. "Goddamn crazy woman." I took this as a compliment. Then his hand started bleeding. He put the flat edge of his fist in his mouth and sucked. "Goddamn fish." He sobbed exactly twice. What a performance. I was transfixed.

"What happened to your hand?" I asked.

"Goddamn fish bit me."

"Let me see."

I took his hand in mine and that was enough to remind me of love, exactly what I'd come here to avoid. I tried to focus on the wound, a small gash, but couldn't stop my thumb from tracing the length of each finger.

"It looks clean," I said.

"I don't know...I can't...." The words came out haltingly, against his will as if pulled by an invisible force. "I don't understand...I was so...careful. But somehow or other—I suspect it's the map, this has never happened to me before—but, it appears...as if...I am lost."

The words, I am lost—they melt me.

We did it on the bear skin in front of the stove. I was on top and Mac hardly moved. Still, it felt good. Mac passed out right after. I thought I'd actually killed him until I found a pulse. I positioned myself inside his embrace, bone against bone, hungry again. What a fool I'd been to think I could do without.

Mac tried to leave, of course. To go back to his family. I missed him, howled in the dark. One night with a man and I'm hooked. The same old story except worse—everything's exaggerated in these woods. Night, winter, love. But then I heard him stumbling through the brush, cursing and moaning. Then silence. Then his head burrowing between my breasts and crying. I held him tight. He tried to leave a few more times but always came back. I admired his determination. Now he just goes fishing.

The next one, Kip, just barged right in.

"Wow, what a cool cabin." I don't think he expected to find me lying there. "Holy shit," he said. Later, he told me he thought I was dead. Kip's a youngster—well-read, idealistic and inexperienced in the ways of the wild. His pack was stuffed with candy and games. He tried to give me mouth-to-mouth resuscitation so I kissed him. Then we fucked and ate Milky Way bars.

Kip can juggle small balls with his feet. He knows all the Vice-Presidents. He likes to tease me, call me Mom. I laugh, then cry. I don't know why. I never tell them my name. They can call me whatever they want.

Kip left twice. The first time because he ran out of candy. The second time he called me an old hag. I cackled for him and he stormed out. Then he decided he liked being lost. "I've never been lost before," he told me. "I grew up in Providence, in a brick house on the corner. We played lots of Scrabble. I know all the two-letter words—once I scored 642 points." I refuse to play. I have to kick him out to get some sleep.

Sleeping and fucking. It's not a bad life. Sometimes it's hard to tell the difference between the two. One blends with the other like the pulse and pause of the heart.

So much has fallen away, become unimportant. I lay supine and the world surrounds me with its riches—I am its queen. Things that have never been imagined happen to me on a regular basis. Ten hands, five lips, then I lose count.

Sammy calls me Lucille. He has long hair and a mustache and plays the guitar. Like me, he is insatiable. He makes love like a river. Sometimes he cries but won't say why. There is an old man who sits in the corner mumbling to himself. He's never touched me but I want him to.

There are others—they keep streaming in—but I've forgotten their names and remember only certain distinguishing characteristics: an accent, a missing finger, a unique rhythm. One man turns into another then another until I can't tell the difference. Or they pile up and I gasp for air.

In rare moments of solitude, when the men go away—to where, I don't know—I wonder, have I let go of too much? I picture the mountains and the valley and the lake—so much wallpaper now—and the trees, an extravagant lace. Somewhere there used to be movies, flowers, wine—paltry substitutes for this endless coming. My body is racked with pleasure. There's a constant burning and I am so thirsty. If only someone would bring me water. It's too much but not enough. Don't stop. Come back. I have, once again, forgotten how to be alone.

Then I hear weeping from the rafters. Someone has left behind a little girl. I can't see her because the candle burnt out but she nibbles on cookies. I know this because the crumbs fall on me. I want to talk to her, to tell her everything is going to be okay but the words get stuck in the back of my throat and the little girl keeps crying. I am wet with tears. I know I should stop this fucking, build a ladder and save her. But I can't remember how to do any of those things. Besides, it's too dark and I can't find my black dress so I decide to wait until daybreak.

Daybreak never comes.

Your Silent Face

By David Ryan

The last time I saw him, the time before, I didn't really see him. I mean, there was his house and I was driving by, and I suppose the house was enough to bring his face to mind. His college face, from years before. From when you and I could say we knew him. This was several years ago. You were still alive and we were together—we had our own concerns and worries, but we were together. Those concerns were nothing, now, looking back.

We'd heard he'd moved to Austin after college, had gotten into oil speculation. And I had been in Austin for work, for a couple of days, so I looked him up. He'd asked after you. Why don't you come by? he said.

I said sure, and I meant it. I drove to the address he'd given me, but in the end I didn't stop. I can't remember if I'd told you. There was a new Audi in the driveway. The house was too large for its yard, the architecture clownish and ostentatious. Like those strip malls dressed up as Mediterranean villas. But, still, the place evoked a sense of comfort and financial security, suggested peril held back for a time. Our lives then, yours and mine, they seemed so full of peril: the exhausted second mortgage, our infant daughter's health, the schools we couldn't afford for her someday.

And so I drove past and kept going. I came back to the hotel and called, apologized. I couldn't get away. Next time, for sure, I said.

I'd forgotten all of this. This was such a minor thing, and I'm only mentioning it for reasons I'll try to explain. But, really, they're reasons I can't explain. I can only gesture around them and hope. I hadn't much experience with this silent flux. The way the unexpected suddenly rises up and makes everything around it small.

I'd forgotten all of this—until recently, because he'd made the news. Something to do with that oil speculation but also with fraud. Fracking, actually—duped investors, falsified geological charts, kickbacks, dodgy loans. He'd pounded a bunch of lies into the earth and made a lot of money.

But then he got caught. And then he called. Called here. Just a couple of days ago. When I picked up and answered a voice said: Wow, man, listen to you! Wow.

And I said: Who is this?

Jesus, Dave. Morgan! the voice said. Morgan!

I thought about every Morgan there was, because there weren't many.

Handley, he said.

Handley—and I saw that house again, saw his much younger face from college.

Morgan, I said, and I thought *why?* I was home with Clare, we'd just come back from ballet. The eight and nine-year-olds were rehearsing to be wildflowers for the August recital. Clare's interest in dance had intensified last winter while playing one of the mice in a production of The Nutcracker. I recall sitting with you during the performance. That night, we hadn't heard anything. There was no reason to think you weren't fine. We hadn't learned what was deeply embedded still in the unknowable. And so that night we watched Clare under the lights, carelessly, this mouse among the prima ballerinas' jetés and pliés, their slender backs and poised arms and spinning legs. We lived in that brilliant ignorance, that momentary glory. We watched dazzled by our daughter's light, unaware that something dark and silent was already moving through you.

On the phone Morgan said: This may sound strange. I need to see you. Could you come out?

And I said, *Yes*. Without understanding why. Maybe *yes* wanted to know how he'd ruined his life. Was he going to jail? I suppose *yes* wanted to know, wanted to feel better about my own life. Morgan had introduced you to me. After college you and I married, moved to Baton Rouge to be closer to your parents. You settle into the distance between the then and now. A kind of silence opens around you. A face, a sound or color, a gesture rises up and shudder, then slinks off back into the dark. Morgan had introduced you to me. Maybe this was really what *yes* wanted to remember. *Yes* wanted this more than anything.

This time, he gave me a different address. I brought Clare to your parents the next morning. And then I drove.

You and I were at an airport, back in college. We were travelling to meet my parents, travelling to Illinois. We were waiting in the terminal, killing time, and you went to get a bottle of water. I watched you walk away, but kept watching. You circled a couple of shops far off. I watched your posture, your way of walking, how you paused to look at a magazine. The smallest gesture of your hand felt so consequential. And then you came back. Nothing had happened, really. I was this voyeur, watching you move through a silence that already knew us both so well. The way a band of light knows all the dust turning inside it. We were killing time, but I didn't know what that meant. Time, we didn't think about it so much.

I drove, stopped a couple of times, drove. Off the highway, three dead wellheads towered over a vast, abandoned fracking lot. Was this one of Morgan's frauds, one of his ghouls? A tumbleweed skipped and bounded over the concrete expanse, rose twirling in the air higher and higher. A black dot, a turkey buzzard, pulled from a sleeve of sky, dropped and attacked the tumbleweed idiotically, mid-air.

Then the exit crumbled to gravel, shot out into bad land, erratic rocks and weeds burst up through veins of clay. The place ahead looked abandoned. Like a compound where a cult once lived. A tall chain link fence surrounded the property. A couple of scrub oaks and cedar elms reached down, scoring the ground, as if scavenging for hope. I pulled up, got out of my car. The fence was high enough to keep strangers out, but who would want to wander into a place like this? There was a large shack with a corrugated tin roof. An open garage attached to it, just a lean-to, a roof with three walls really. Inside, I saw that Audi of his; now up on blocks, a back wheel missing. And beside it an old sofa.

I pressed the intercom button in the gate. A cloud of fruit flies hovered, as if the box had exhaled them. Far off, two white dots were fused to the surface of a pond reflecting streaks of orange and platinum under the setting sky. I pressed the intercom button again. I wished I was back home with Clare.

The two white dots on the pond were slowly moving over the water, now on land. I pushed the button again. The white dots were coming toward me. Their shapes clarified into swans. Static noise came from the intercom. The swans were skimming the ground now, half-flying towards me. Then they were only a few feet away. I hit the buzzer, then jumped back as the swans reared and slapped at the chain link. A man came out of the house. He didn't look like Morgan. He lifted a coiled hose from the porch, shot a blast of water at the swans. They flapped and screamed in the rainbow spray, then scuttled back toward the pond.

Sorry, he shouted—now, I barely recognized his face—They're like that. He opened the gate. Look at you, he said. Man it's good to see you.

You too, I said and we embraced like old friends. We passed a bunch of little chrome machines piled on the ground like tiny robots. He saw me looking at them. Tattoo guns, he said. Tattoo artist lived here, everyone knew him. Taught classes. But then he just vanished. I got this for almost nothing.

He was breathing heavy, like the short distance between the gate and his front door had exerted him. And his walking was unsteady. He'd maybe already been drinking. The weight he'd put on, the bloat in his face—I wouldn't have recognized him had I not known who he was supposed to be.

As we stepped up onto the porch I felt this unsteadiness, then the boards of the floor started to tremble then shudder. My arms reached out, grabbing at air for balance. Then the shuddering stopped.

I did that, he said, and then he laughed.

What? I said. In the distance the swans were airborne, hovering over the pond.

Bad joke, he said. Just a tremor. They're nothing. You get used to it. They're like the coyotes and wolves here. At night, all over the place. You get used to them too. Even those swans have gotten used to them.

The news about him, I thought. All the horizontal drilling, the punctured striated layers of shale. The industry geologists had known, hadn't they? That it could be like this? But they had made a lot of money too.

Inside, the house smelled like a dive bar. The sofa was expensive, out of place here. On the coffee table there was a pizza box and bottle of Laphroaig.

Home, he said. Hey, how's Kate—you still hanging in there?

Yeah, I said, though I don't know why. She's with Clare. Clare's our daughter.

A daughter, he said. Wow. I set you and Kate up! Remember? That's Jeanine over there.

There, on a table beneath the window, was a photograph: the two of them dressed up, smiling, teeth white, tanned faces.

Yeah, we were engaged. But—well, after everything fell apart, he said. You heard about that, right?

95

Heard about what? I said, which was a lie, like saying that you were home with Clare. But where was the currency of truth in this room? He poured us both a scotch and I didn't tell him I didn't drink anymore. There was a pack of cigarettes on the table and a red lighter. I didn't smoke anymore, either. But that wouldn't stop me here.

Yeah, he said. He handed me my glass. I got involved with some mining deals. But it got messy. It went from messy to ugly to a kind of larceny, I guess. Know. I mean, I know. I know only too well.

We sat and he told me a version of what I'd already heard, but with certain details about the drilling added and certain other details missing. He poured his scotch to the top of the tumbler, drink after drink. I soon forgot why I'd come here. He was talking about the money coming in until it was ridiculous and profane. I had everything covered, he said. Like, I *knew* what could go wrong. The risks.

The room had gotten dark. He turned on a lamp and returned to the sofa. But I didn't, he said. I mean, you see. You see you don't know anything, really.

His landline rang and a woman's voice, Jeanine I assumed, recited the recorded greeting. Then there was just a dial tone.

Yeah, he said. But I'm okay now. I had a good lawyer. Some fines. No jail time. But I'm a local celebrity now. They all know what I am. They think they do.

He set his glass down on the table and stared at it a moment, then looked up. I might go back to Arizona, he said. You remember Jaime?

Oh yeah, I said.

He's got a savings and loan, says he'd have a job for me in a year or so. When my fifteen minutes blows over. Oh. Hold on.

He stood and paused, as if mistrusting the space around him. Then he went upstairs. Beneath the table by the window with the picture of the happy, tan couple was an arrangement of glass bottles, big and small, clear and brown and pale blue and green. A little candy-colored family. A dozen glass children, beneath the photograph

96

of what would have been his wife. In the wall, water rushed through the plumbing and his feet creaked down the stairs.

I've been having the strangest dreams, he said, returning to the sofa. You ever have this? The dream is just life? Like, I go to my office and have a conversation with my assistant. We'll talk about the weather, or about her kid who's on the spectrum. I have a nice lunch. I mean, I don't fly or fall from the sky. I'm not naked in public. I don't wake in love with some stranger I'll never meet. I don't wake terrified, or embarrassed. Or humbled. I just wake.

I wake, he said: Here.

The bottles on the floor began chattering. Like the ground was welling up in laughter, like he'd just told a joke. My chair trembled beneath me, too, laughing.

Hold on, he said. It's fine. It's okay. He took a wobbly sip of his scotch. It spilled down his chin onto his shirt. Something upstairs fell and crashed. Then the air calmed and it was quiet and still again.

Mindfulness, he said. And looked at me but his eyes, glassy and unfocussed, had lost their gaze. He muttered something. I wondered: had he just gotten used to this lately, a show without an audience? We'll all be dead, he said, before it's too late. He stood, then sat back down.

He waved his hand, as if at a fly. He laid back on the sofa and fell asleep. I sat there in the silence. I kept expecting you to come down the stairs, as if you had come here with me. Or maybe Morgan would wake and say, Kate, this is David. David, this is Kate.

I went upstairs, as if to find you. In the bathroom on the sink there were several opened bottles of pills. The whites and blues and greens recalled all the medication you'd had to take, eventually. I heard a baby cry out, a fox or a coyote or some kind of cat. But before I realized what it was, it was a baby.

Downstairs, Morgan's body seemed to have melted on the sofa. I took a cigarette from the pack and his lighter and went out the front door.

Out in the dark sky, stars punched thick, brilliant dots into vapors of red, blue, and gold—these other galaxies impossibly far away. No one could touch those, I thought. No one could jam them up. I came around to the garage to Morgan's broken Audi, the old sofa there with its springs shot up through the upholstery. I smoked and the cigarette dizzied me, swelled inside me with a kind of false joy. Far off, the swans were silhouetted under the moon.

I didn't feel right to drive, though I was drunk enough to remember I had my keys and think about it. It would be better to go back inside, sleep for a while.

But when I tried the garage door that led inside, it was locked. I went around front. The door was locked, too. So I knocked and waited. I looked into the window. Morgan's body had half-slipped off the sofa, head and shoulders on the floor. His arms were outstretched like they intended to catch something enormous falling down on him.

I pulled my face back and saw you. You were reflected in the glass. Your silent face.

In the garage I laid down on the sofa. I reached out and touched the expensive car. I saw my breath and closed my eyes.

But later, I don't know how much, I woke and heard myself laughing. I couldn't remember why, but something was moving in the garage. Or maybe I had simply woken up a dream that had been waiting for me. But as I lay there this dark thing, this dream, brushed against me. I stayed there, frozen. I smelled its breath. Something, a muzzle came near my face, then its heat fell away. It shuffled off, out of the garage. Then there was just my brain pulsing the sounds formed in the vacuum of my body.

I got up, opened Morgan's car door and climbed inside.

When I woke again the sun was rising. I went around front. Through the window, Morgan lay sprawled out as he'd been hours ago. I remembered my phone and tried his number. The voice of

Jeanine picked up and asked me to leave a message after the tone. Her voice, a ghost on a machine. What did they mean to each other now?

Morgan. Wake up, I said. Wake up, you asshole. The last time I'd seen him was back in college. Probably the last. The last in my memory. He was like this, blacked out on a sofa. Between then and now nothing had changed, just this, so many years.

I never liked you, Morgan, I said into the phone. Still he didn't stir.

But you *are* here, aren't you? Maybe now you're a molecule in a deer or a dog or one of those ancient irises that rises up each spring in our garden after we thought it had died for good last fall. Maybe you can hear what I'm saying, can hear even the thoughts that pass silently inside my intuition, my instincts. Sometimes I worry that Clare hears me talking to myself, worries her father has lost control over our lives. That she will see too soon that I'm not worthy of her trust. I don't want her to know all that I can't protect her from.

The last thing you said, you said, *You've caught me at a bad time.* And you tried to laugh. Your eyes that moment, you could barely keep them open. It wasn't a bad time, it was all time. Now it was. Every moment is the only time.

A day or two after Clare was born, we were driving home from the hospital. And that silence had entered the car. At a stop I glanced at you and was in that moment a kind of voyeur again. Your silent face. The exhaustion in your eyes and mouth. The delivery had been difficult. How strange, that childbirth rides so recklessly on the edge of death. All that can go wrong. Now, in this glance, the world was returning to us. Something had been answered in our lives, to which we'd never known the question. And in which the answer was itself a terrifying set of new questions, of possibilities. Questions faceted like a jewel.

In that glance I suspected you were thinking this too. That nothing had happened yet. The past had lost its charge. We'd reached the *now* of our lives. Old truths about us were shearing away—truth, doubling, reversing, washing up on the shore of each moment. The present now was the truth. The most fragile truth.

Your eyes then, too, you could barely keep them open. How young you looked. So tired but so young. I couldn't have known then how clearly you could appear to me now. Couldn't have known this reversal, now, of what seemed so new then. Now, a single synapse might spark the past and send it cascading through a labyrinth of associations into the hardened present. How easily memory now blows up and obliterates the present. Exerts its pressure.

We die and that pressure releases into someone we love, into their body. This galaxy of potential memory. We vanish into those we loved. In some small moment, someone remembers us from when we were living. And we're alive again. A star's light blazes, though it has been dead for years. You're such a young star.

I knocked again.

The two white dots on the runoff pond had gone black. It was just the sunrise casting shadows from the other side of the earth.

I knocked once more. But, really, I couldn't wait to get home. I got in my car and drove.

Limbs

By Liz Matthews

By mid-November 1954, the last of the leaves let go. A stray yellow-ish Maple leaf wafted on the back patio. The bumblebees retreated, finished with their seasonal work. The way the sun hit the grass was different—more confrontational. Maggie had spent the morning writing in her sun porch. After a few hours, her fingers cramped, and her head throbbed from dredging up the past.

She pushed away from her typewriter and faced the mass of paperwork that had taken over her desk. As she shuffled a bundle of pages from one pile to the next, she unearthed an insurance form that had come in the mail a few days before:

Patient Margaret Bourke-White

Age: 50

Diagnosis: Parkinson's disease

Parkinson's. Parkinson's. Not an illness. A disease. The latter was worse. The latter had no cure. This was the disease that Edward Weston had suffered from. What had Captain Steichen said about Weston? "Terrible. Just terrible. Especially for a photographer. Everything seizes up. You can't move, you can't use your limbs, you become a prisoner in your own body."

Disease. A word she'd used so flippantly about herself. In Italy, she'd told her assistant that war correspondents have the *disease* of being afraid to miss out on any action. She put her life in danger for the best shot, never imagined it would be her own body that betrayed her.

Though she wanted to rip the paper and throw it in the fireplace, what good would that do? She couldn't burn the disease.

Instead, she walked to the opposite end of the house to assure herself that her limbs still worked. The route was circuitous. Up a few stairs to the living room, down a few more to the dining room, through the swinging door into the kitchen, left into the den. Next, out the side door to breathe in the fresh air, to get out of her head. Yes, she could still move, but her arms wouldn't swing unless she told them to. And her gait was stilted, interrupted. What would this disease actually do to her body? To her mind?

Outside, the warmth of sun loosened her gait. Point O' Woods Road South and its surrounding suburban roads were ideal for walking. She walked the perimeter of the yard and ran her fingers along the jagged tree trunks. She inhaled the earthy smell of the fallen leaves and let the fresh air work its way into her bloodstream. Pausing at the birdbath, she listened for birds or other signs of life, but all the living creatures concealed themselves. Where were the goldfinches? The wrens? Where were the deer and their does that grazed in her grass?

Where were her Purple Heart Valley pictures? 1944. Cassino Valley, Italy. The surgeons at work with Nurse Barnes by their side, who'd learned all the Texan soldiers' names. Who tended to a transfusion needle during shell bombing right outside the tent. The nurses beneath their cots as the creeping barrage of enemy fire closed in. And after the film arrived at the Pentagon, it had disappeared somewhere between the dark room and the censorship.

If the pool weren't just covered for the season, Maggie would have gone for a swim. Instead, she walked, then marched, towards the front yard, towards her tiger lilies that lay dormant until next summer, along with the rhododendrons, dogwoods, bleeding hearts, and mountain laurels.

She was not a prisoner yet. But what kind of life lay ahead for her?

Though she had already taken a long walk earlier that morning, she turned down her driveway, and started again. She couldn't go back inside to face that piece of paper with her fate. She'd stalk the property and plan her house series.

Lately, during her walks she'd pitch forward. The weight of her body pulled her towards the ground. She counteracted with longer steps. This time, her foot plunged into one of the deeper potholes and before she could stop it, she stumbled over her trapped foot and collapsed beside the hole.

On the ground, she traced the pothole with her finger.

Cassino, Italy, where shell holes filled with water littered the valley and dotted the landscape like these potholes. She'd joined Captain Jack Marinelli on a flying mission to seek out a German mortar that plagued the American soldiers. They flew above the tips of the mountaintops and in the crests between, far above the plumes of white smoke that followed the bombs, above the demolished bridges and the replacements that the engineers had constructed besides them. Maggie, in the observation seat with unprecedented access for her cameras.

Especially for a photographer.

In a field hospital later that night, Maggie lay on the ground with her Rollei, propped up on her elbows, with peanut lights to get the shots while German shells still went off. The first shell hit the mess hall, only thirty feet from where Maggie, the wounded soldiers, the doctors, and nurses camped out. The bombs dropped without a reliable rhythm throughout the night, close enough they'd have to take cover each time. But the wires for the bulbs stayed intact, and Maggie shot from her supine position. This is what she'd trained for. She shot the suffering soldiers and the brave doctors and nurses who risked their lives to save them.

Finally, she stood up in her driveway and brushed the crumbled concrete off her pants, then kicked the debris back into the hole. So much of her life had depended on being in the right place at the right time. In fact, she'd needed to be in the spot the moments before the action took place. Much of what she shot came out to nothing, but that one photograph that came close to perfection, that was enough to keep calling her back.

That war-torn Italian city was being rebuilt amid its destruction. No, she did not feel scared.

But why did her past insist on visiting her? Was this how the minds of people who didn't travel worked? Now that she was forced to spend more time at home, to focus on her exercises, to get stronger, maybe this montage of her life would become inescapable. And what if each scene presented itself as a last gasp, only to disappear from her memory for good?

She would not allow her body to take her prisoner. Back in the observation seat with the doctors at the wheel, now it was time for her to study the enemy territory, to learn, to take orders, and to once again be the exception. She wasn't the first. Not all adventurous lives were cut short by disease. Life didn't work like that. But if it was a legacy that drove her for so long, that was cemented by now.

The following week, her teenage neighbor Binxy stopped by to borrow the Studebaker again and handed Maggie the prints that his father brought home from the city. She tossed him the keys and moved as fast her body allowed to her living room, where she tore open the package and spread the prints of her home along the floor. She preferred to look at a series this way, together, to take in the story she was trying to tell all at once.

There it stood: her Dutch Colonial home in Connecticut. In each shot, the house loomed, took center stage even among the giant oak trees that circled it. Still, she scanned the prints for some missing element. Was it people or faces? No. She'd shot plenty of landscapes. But something had been wrong. The barren prairies. The Italian mountains ablaze. There was nothing wrong with her home, only that to get these shots it took the same amount of strength and resilience as if she still hung out of helicopter or stayed up all night in a bunker.

She needed to go further back to before the wars. To the days of machines and skyscrapers, to the factories where she shot rows and rows of the same high-heeled shoe, and yet still been satisfied.

How to do the same with just a house? How to present the integrity of her home?

When she stood to consider the prints from a new angle, she stumbled and reached for the wainscoting to steady herself. Her focus interrupted, she turned to face the outside where it sounded like a pack of hounds charged down her street. As she steadied herself, she closed her eyes. Something between a bark and a howl. For a moment, she forgot where she was. When she opened her eyes again, a shadow had fallen over the driveway. Outside, a flock of migrating snow geese flew past—beautiful in their breadth—the way they occupied the sky with such purpose. She imagined shooting these birds from above, with the earth beneath them. But could she handle that anymore? Instead, she looked back at the house.

The birds had all flown away. She couldn't even hear the remnants of their honks.

Inside, she considered the photos again. They were good pictures— she'd used the light well and had presented the roof and dormers through unexpected vantage points. As usual, she'd let her camera guide her. But still the house itself was not enough. This was not the Supreme Court or the Chrysler building. The house existed through her gaze because of what she had put herself through. This house was worth all this work because of what she had suffered through to earn it. What she still fought against to keep it.

Perhaps it was she who was missing.

Alien Fingers

By Eden Marchese

I tried to reach for another soul so I could feel whole. I don't know if that makes sense to anyone else, but I *almost* did it. His name was Paul. It's always a Paul, isn't it? I was swept into his world from his fingers, the way they felt when he ran them up and down my body. The way they felt between my legs, almost like they were reaching for all that I hide away. The way they felt on my tongue. I don't mean to fixate on fingers, I don't have a *fetish*, but Paul's were something from another world. It's what I imagine the aliens that invade us will have for fingers. If the aliens have fingers like his, we'd all submit quietly and fully. They can have the planet, we've fucked it up enough anyway, just let us know why one of their kind hid among us and pretended it was normal to have other-worldly fingers.

I met Paul at a party. Cliché I know, but it's what happened. It even happened like in the movies: Guy sees person enter the dance floor, guy is holding his drink with his alien fingers and the person becomes mesmerized because the guy's eyes are glowing all the colors of the universe. Person is stuck stammering for anything to say as guy comes up to them, giving some kind of greeting under the music's cry for attention, person nods in response even though that isn't the appropriate answer. Guy laughs and repeats greeting, adding in that his name is Paul. Guy's name lights the person's brain on fire as it screams for their lips to touch and person almost responds this time by kissing Guy. Guy, though person knew his name was Paul at this point, repeats the greeting again, this time going *over* the music instead of under—his dominant side taking over in a hope that the person would understand. They understood. Even under the music, I understood him.

Person's brain starts pumping out a response, a laugh thrown in along with some throwaway about the music being loud. The alien fingers brush their own and person feels how those girls in Salem felt all those years ago. *Alive.* Guy—Paul—asks for the person's name, person somehow forgetting this in their brain's quick attempt to keep this creature near them, and person responds.

Our names are now on each other's lips, my name tangled in his tongue and his in mine. We stood and talked about everything yet nothing as the music raged on, as bodies became one around us and as the lights began to come back up. At some point, the alien fingers and the hand they were attached to began to rest on my shoulder. It was mesmerizing. It was like I was watching porn for the first time, the feeling of ecstasy at finishing at the same time the actors did. I was the actor in this porno and his fingers were my opposite. I don't have a *fetish*. I promise you. If you were to see the fingers I'm talking about, you'd be writing novels about them too.

I don't know how long it was before we realized the party was over, even with all we talked about it felt like I didn't know him. I knew his name was Paul Grayson. His eyes are the color of the universe, his fingers alien. He has tree branches for legs and arms, his heart the heat of the stars. He was from a small town in Oklahoma, where all the aliens come from, I'm sure, and he didn't have any family left. This was probably another ploy for his fake story. His mom, Margaret Grayson, died at the age of forty-five. Paul's father didn't have alien fingers. His were human. That's why they held the gun that killed Margaret. It's why his fingers turned on him and put a bullet between his eyes. It's why he didn't die. Paul didn't mention where his father was now, not that it mattered much to me, I was never a "meet the parents" kind of person anyway. Too much stress. I almost counted myself lucky to meet an alien with the equivalent of two dead parents. Almost. It would be rude of me to think that.

He likes his eggs over-easy and blanketed in pepper. He's allergic to mayonnaise. Deathly. Margaret almost killed him when he was a kid, made him a PB&J sandwich with a dash of mayonnaise and he turned purple. His poor fingers must've been panicking at the thought of never being able to touch me. I tear up just thinking about how they must've felt to feel the life slowly leave Paul's body, the relief when the life came rushing back in. This is where Paul says he began to feel alive for the first time. So, from then on, he planned to move to Toronto and become a teacher. Alien Paul a teacher. His students wouldn't be able to comprehend what he was teaching them, how could they? Those little whores would be fixated on *my* fingers. They'd be asking him questions just to see how he flexes his hands when thinking, they'd want to see how he pushes up his glasses when he gets excited, they would be jumping over one another to be the one to make him be excited. Each of their breaths hanging off of that single motion.

All of this to say, I didn't know him then. You can know all of this about a person but still not *know* them. It's why he didn't know me, though we would play our game some nights when we lay together in bed. The game was simple. List all you could remember about the other person. The longer list won the game and the winner got to choose the next day's activity. This was when he would push his glasses up the most. Each time he'd see me smile; glasses pushed up. Each time I laughed; glasses pushed up. Each time I cried; glasses pushed up. Anyway: the game. Hearing him list everything he remembered about me gave me the same feeling when I saw him the first time.

Each time, he'd start by smiling and saying: "Well, Mx. Grayson," he always would pretend we were married, "what do I know about you? This is a hard one..." and he'd feign ignorance while looking around the room. As if the answers were anywhere but my eyes. My eyes gave the most away about anything I was thinking. If he were to reach into my eyes, not my body, he'd find all that I try to hide.

He'd find it illuminated and alphabetized for his reading pleasure. There'd be a coffee table with his favorite tea, *Jasmine*, at the perfect temperature for him and it would stay that way until he was done reading everything. "What do I know about you?" he would say, "I know many things. I know you're a Taurus but you like to say you're a Gemini, that you're from Milan, your family moved here when you were nineteen and you've lived in Oklahoma ever since. You want to be a singer and write beautiful songs, one even played on the radio once though you are still nervous to send out anything new. Your fingers are littered with the little scars of a guitarist. You have one sister named Mace, short for Macedonia because your parents are weird, and you love her to death even when she drives you crazy. Your favorite color is brown, like my eyes." I never corrected him on this one since his eyes were *not* brown. I tried to tell him about how his eyes held the universe, but he looked at me weird and laughed. I joined in to comfort him, I didn't want my seriousness to push something so perfect away. "Your favorite ice cream is chocolate with Nutella though you stopped eating it since I'm allergic." He was always wrong here too; he was allergic to mayonnaise—not anything in my ice cream choices. I rarely corrected him during these games, and it was always easier to let him win than to argue about what he knew about me.

There is a certain comfort and power that comes from knowing more about your partner than they do you, even after a year together. It wasn't a competition, at least knowingly, and I always loved him the same by the end. Whenever I'd win the game, which I could do easily and without much effort, we'd go on adventures together, increasingly outrageous things thrown in to get Paul to laugh or smile. Our favorite adventure, the one he laughed the most on, was when we went to the Grand Canyon. Drove the whole way. He doesn't like to drive much so I humored him and made sure to be perfect the whole time in the car. He has a sensitive stomach, something the aliens he was sent by didn't account for when under the climate in the western United States. Our music taste was the one thing we didn't agree on in our time together, so we would usually listen to different podcasts.

This trip's: aliens. The whole drive, I was torn between making sure we didn't swerve off of the road and connecting the dots between different alien experiences and why Paul's fingers were anything but human. Human fingers hurt things, his never have. It didn't add up, it wasn't *sane*. Paul laughed at each of the "ridiculous," his words, not mine, people who he said were high and didn't realize they were still tripping off whatever they took. I wasn't so convinced; why would an alien admit to the stories anyway? One girl, a devout Catholic, claimed that she saw aliens while outside watering her garden. She said a man came up to her fence and she knew right away he was an alien. Do you want to know what gave it away? Her finger fetish. Even the Catholics can be gross like that, her obsession with fingers, I mean. She admitted it right on air for the whole world to know.

People like her were disturbed, but her story was important. She spent her whole life obsessed with people's fingers and knew a human's from an other-worldly creature's. This is how I knew my observation wasn't baseless. Paul hated the woman. He tried to play it off as a disdain for the Catholics that tried to show him what they believed love was, but I knew it was because she pointed out what others forgot. The fingers.

I felt bad seeing Paul upset and didn't want him to leave before we got to the cliffside, so I put on some of his music. He laughed when it began to play and looked like *I* was the alien. Can you imagine that? I laugh now whenever I remember how his face looked. His glasses were being pushed up the rest of the drive as we went through each of his favorite songs. I couldn't help but be brought into the energy and sang along with him from time-to-time which only made the both of us laugh more because I was *terrible* and he was beautiful. I was human. I think I hated him a little bit that day, knowing that he could sing perfectly because he was lucky enough to be from an alien race with perfect fingers and perfect vocal cords.

The Grand Canyon was beautiful, not that it was a shock to either of us. No one goes there thinking they're about to be underwhelmed. Even aliens know the beauty of the place they're standing. Paul wanted to take pictures; he didn't care that my human fingers would be touching the screen of his phone, he didn't care that my human lips were touching his name. He forced me to take a couple with him. "What kind of couple doesn't take photos together?" was his reasoning. It was the first time he said we were together like I always thought we were. It felt like he was completing a sentence I have been trying to finish my whole life. We were one the whole rest of the trip: whenever Paul took a picture, I was attached to his hip. When his lips moved, mine moved to stay in time. When his fingers brushed me hungrily, mine echoed and led him into the bathroom.

The stall was our own dance floor. It felt like we were meeting one another for the first time, his fingers everywhere as if they needed to decode every cell in my body. Mine were stuck gripping the steel of the door but I didn't mind. Sometimes, some of my fingers would be allowed to touch him. It was touching him that let me feel what the aliens would feel like when we first would shake their hands. I'll be able to watch the event unfold on TV and say, with confidence, that I know what that feels like. My humanness betrayed him just as the aliens would be betrayed by the rest of our vileness eventually. I was gripping the door as he tried to save my human body from the curse deep within me and my left hand slipped from its place. I didn't have time to react, I *couldn't* react, as I watched my hands try to grasp onto something, Paul being pulled with my orbit. Even after all this time, I can't fathom how it happened. How my orbit could have pulled such a beautiful being as I did, how he fell with clipped wings and had to touch his hands to our dance floor in order to stop himself from falling completely. No matter how many times the scene plays

111

in my head, nothing I do can stop my foot from slamming down on the very tools my savior needed for me. In my rush to get back to satisfying my vile hunger, *Paul* cried out and pulled his hand towards him. *Paul* was my humanity's casualty. I watched his alien fingers for signs of death, his voice low as the dance floor collapsed.

The drive home, I couldn't stop looking at my fingers. My left hand. I hated them for defacing *my* alien. They tore at what was supposed to be felt only by other aliens. My vile human fingers could be what spread some disease to him and kill him if I'm not careful. Who knows what kinds of diseases will unfold that the aliens didn't know about? If I was the one who brought the end of Paul's life, I wouldn't be able to keep going. I knew that deep down and was on the verge of pushing him out of the car so I could ram myself into a sixteen-wheeler to save us both the trouble. I decided to cut my fingers off on the traitorous hand. This was the only proper punishment I could think of for a thing as disgusting as that hand. I need to hold back the urge to spit just thinking about it.

Whenever Paul would win the game, he'd want us to relax for the day. I didn't blame him so much, my adventures could be tiresome, but it did get boring to be home for more than two hours. He'd be holed up in the living room with something on TV that we agreed to watch together. I could never keep up with his shows, they were always so dark. So creepy. He said he liked the feeling of being chilled to his bone, of being so horrified he wouldn't be able to respond. I didn't have the stomach for it. Especially the ones that were more on the violent side. These were the rules though: the winner of the game, even if I *let* him win, was allowed to choose what we did for the day. He wouldn't hold me to it too much though, he understood my aversion to violence. I still had bruises when he met me, after all.

But now we were here, almost two years into his finger's invasion of my body, a week after my hand's betrayal, and I let him win five days in a row. I don't know why, but I got a little bit drunk on his smile that week. It pulled me down into his arms, pulled me away from the violence of the world and made me feel like I was lying between the stars. I should've known it was the last week we would be together. That's always how these things work, isn't it? It was the fifth day of him choosing to relax inside. We were cuddled up next to one another on the couch while watching some murder mystery movie. It wasn't as bad as the others so I was able to stay most of the runtime. I was hungry though and should've dealt with this before sitting down next to Paul. He never helped when I was hungry. It was like his heart's fire would bleed into me and encourage me to be *ravenous*.

This was why I couldn't control my left hand as it slid under the blanket and ate at him. His glasses fogged up a bit in response, his smile making me want to believe it was okay but I could only feel disgust. The traitor hand was lucky the first time that I was in a car when contemplating its punishment, the punishment then being me sitting on it the rest of the drive so it felt what Paul felt when poisoned by Margaret. Now, *my* Paul was being eaten alive by this hunger-driven madness and he was enjoying it. He was enjoying that I was stuck not being able to touch him, to feel him. His alien fingers were on either side of him, glaring at me as I let the traitor have its way with the one that I loved. The one with the universe for eyes, the one allergic to mayonnaise, the one who would be watched by hungry eyes wherever he went, as if those eyes knew the foreign beauty that graced their existence.

Before I could think to use the hand that I still had control over to stop this inappropriate act, it was over. Paul was panting and smiled at me. Challenged me. He asked me to get a towel—he knew what he was doing. I nodded and got up, hoping his alien fingers would follow me. They didn't. They were disgusted with me and I under-stood why. It's why I walked into the kitchen, the cutting board still out from the celery Paul was cutting up before, and grabbed the knife. It's why I didn't listen to the traitor's vile cries as it begged for forgiveness. I smiled as I watched each of the fingers fall away. It was a beautiful sight. It was like the knife was Paul when he first saw me, cutting through all the vileness in my life and bringing me into a new light. A new me.

I heard Paul come into the kitchen behind me as he was saying something under the screams from the TV. I didn't hear him until he repeated the question, making a joke about how loud the TV was. I turned around to look at my beautiful creature. I watched his universe-filled eyes glance towards the punished traitor. I watched as he took in how my hand was *finally* free of its sin. The whole world was still in this moment. It was then that I knew the world only existed for this being. For this *moment*.

His alien fingers moved his glasses up his nose.

Sanctuary

By Jaclyn Gilbert

It is dark when the train pulls into the station. Barbara hears ticking, and there is a sign rolling out departure and arrival times. Track numbers.

Inside the main terminal, people hurry about their luggage and shopping bags. They grab small packs of food and bottled beverages. Potato chips, hard pretzels, and cans of soda—the same brands Rosalie sold at the auction house snack stand. There is a rack of postcards. Barbara sees pictures of her own people in buggies, on horse-drawn plows. Same as the photographs in the Lancaster market, but there are more pictures to choose from here. Or perhaps it is that she has never stopped to look at her people up close. All the time she's forbidden herself pause. Busying herself with Eli, with the farm, and preparing food for her husband.

Stay here, she thinks. God, may I find strength, she prays.

She peers into the photographs, holds onto each image. Men plowing the fields under a setting sun. Women hanging clotheslines to dry. Buggies entering and leaving covered bridges. A close up of a small girl with blond braids wrapped around her head. Her eyes innocent and unknowing as her youngest daughter Emma's once were. Her only surviving daughter.

Emma had been living in the city for over a year now; she had a child, Barbara's grandson, in this place packed with the noise of people chasing trains. Barbara did not know the first thing about the city—about Philadelphia—and so when she saw a stand with maps in long folded columns, she reached for one to buy.

English faces watch her. It takes the woman behind the counter a moment to give her change, which Barbara folds back into her envelope and places in her bag.

In the central terminal, she opens the map in her lap, tracing roads and rivers in red and blue, like the veins of a body, she thinks. Like the anatomy chart Doctor Caldwell kept in his office. She tried to memorize the parts of the heart, once, while the doctor took Eli's blood. The words *ventricle* and *artery* entered her, words she clings to now, without realizing. The roads are bloodlines, she thinks, for the innerworkings of her brain and lungs. *The spinal column*, a body part she's always found beautiful, she thinks, as she traces her finger still further down the map to learn the divisions of the city. Her hands are trembling.

You must be brave, she tells herself, turning to the small slip of paper with the name of the real estate agent Mrs. Caldwell gave her. *Eveline Mitchell*, along with her phone number and office address. *456 Walnut Street.* She studies her route on the map. There is a key for measuring miles as inches. It is a long way to Walnut Street, close to five miles. She's walked much longer in her lifetime, but never in a city as big as this. She cannot fathom the extent of her own terror, the way it comes upon her again no matter how many times she tries to quiet it.

By the exit to the street, headlights flicker red. Street lamps beckon. You have time, Barbara tells herself. Take your time.

She follows names of roads she'd written out on the back of the paper with Eveline's address. She'll find a hotel on Walnut Street, a main city road that was supposed to contain what she would need. Barbara will walk from the hotel to Eveline's real estate office in the morning. After she'd left the community with no chance of return, Emma had found a home with Eveline's help. Emma had been baptized and still she had left her family, her mother, who would have done everything in her power to keep her safe.

Barbara walks slowly through the streets. She stops at every street sign, confirming its name on a map. She waits for a streetlight to illuminate the right words. A flicker of black print on white, in the dark. The streets are busy. The English walk quickly. Cars in traffic blare their horns. A mile in, Barbara passes more restaurants and bars. Laughter passes along the sidewalk, people holding cigarettes. Little bits of red fire in the night. A quarter of a mile later, there is a large sign, the shimmer of a fish with claws. RED LOBSTER, it says. The claws are enormous, a devil's grin. Barbara's legs tremble as she walks. It is ten o'clock by the time she reaches Walnut Street. No Holiday Inn illuminating the night like she imagines. But there is a small corner grocery store. Inside, it's crammed with stacks of packaged food and soda pop. Magazines and candy bars. Boxes of cigarettes behind the register where a man sits half-shielded in bullet-proof glass. She knows it exists because she read about it after the shooting, the kind of glass that might have kept her children safe. There had been no warning when the milkman came, and her two girls, Beth and Emma, had been there. Beth who had offered her life first because she was the eldest, following *Martyrs Mirror*, according to tradition.

"Can I help you?" the man at the register asks.

Barbara is still holding her bag, yet her hands felt empty. She almost reaches for a candy bar to buy. She is not certain how far her money will go.

"Do you know the Holiday Inn?" she asks. "Where it is?"

"Holiday Inn," he pauses, as if he is trying to picture one nearby. "Not that I know of," he says. He smiles, yellow teeth. *Cigarettes, nicotine*, words she's only ever heard in passing.

"Do Amish folk like hotels?" His voice is raspy, as though ill with cold and fever. God have mercy on this man, she prays. When Barbara opens her mouth to speak, she feels a hand on her shoulder. She turns to find a young boy. A teenager in a green baseball cap.

"It's not far," he says. "A few blocks south. Make a right out of here and then another right on thirty-eighth street. Keep walking and you'll see a big sign for it. All lit up," he says.

"Good luck," the man at the register laughs.

Barbara thanks the boy. She whispers these directions under her breath as she walks. When she sees the sign, she sighs, but then as she reaches into her bag for the envelope, it has lost its thickness. She hurries to open it, and the fold of bills is gone. She kneels to search every inch of her bag, feeling in and out of the space around her map and the shawl she'd almost forgotten she'd packed. She checks her apron pockets, patting along them, in case she'd hidden the money somewhere else and forgotten. She retraces her steps from when she'd first packed the money out of the sock she'd been hiding in the dresser drawer, and then early this morning before church she'd slipped it into one of the envelopes they kept in the drawer of the hutch. She'd packed the envelope into the bag with her shawl after she left the service and went to the cellar with the pie, but maybe when she ran out of Sara's house, the envelope had fallen out? No—she'd had it on the train—she'd checked after she'd taken her seat and kept the bag on her lap.

But then maybe the man—there had been a man in a suit, his hair black and shiny—who had glanced at her. Maybe he'd been watching and waiting until she'd fallen asleep. She had slept for a few moments—or was it longer, enough time for the man to slip the envelope out of her bag without her noticing? Such thoughts continue to consume her, until she forces them to stop.

Lord, Father, she prays. Please, forgive me. I have made a mistake. I was careless. Father, will you forgive me? Then the thought comes to her, as if the Lord Himself were telling her what to do. There was no shame asking for help. The voice is strong, the Lord's voice, rising up within her. May a stranger take mercy on me and help me find shelter.

She stands on the corner, under the dim lights of a streetlamp outside of the hotel, waiting for another woman, another mother like her—someone who might take pity on her and offer a place to sleep? But the longer she waits, there is only a man, and then a teenager with headphones hurrying past her, indifferent to her standing there. The half-illumined faces of more passersby cross her there on the corner, and she asks nothing of them. She hugs her shawl around her; she'll walk. Stay on the main avenue until she sees a sign for an inn, or a hotel—or a motel? She was never certain of the difference.

She doesn't know how long she walks until she spots one, bright red and glowing, in the distance. She quickens her feet, already blistering against Mrs. Caldwell's thick leather sandals. The hotel had to be a large building to warrant such bright lights, she thinks. She imagines hundreds of rooms stacked on top of one another, each containing beds with pressed sheets and bathrooms with pressed towels. Never mind the television set and telephone for ordering room service like she heard Mrs. McPherson explain once while she was cleaning. How good the room service could be at a four-star hotel. Barbara never required such luxuries. She only needed a bed, a safe room to sleep in, as when Mary and Joseph settled for a stable when all the inns were full.

But when Barbara reaches the flashing red light, it only says PARKING GARAGE with the cost to park per hour. She guesses it's at least midnight by now, and there aren't any cars entering the building. When she peers down through the mouth of the garage, she doesn't see any attendants either. She smells gas and hears the dripping of pipes somewhere far off.

She teeters in past an empty booth for collecting payment and is relieved not to be seen. But almost as soon as she thinks this, she hears a man yelling something to another man about a certain kind of car. A Toyota SUV, they say. She looks around but the men's voices are just echoes scattered through the labyrinth of rusted concrete, so she starts to run up the bend that seems to wind and wind as she looks up and realizes the depth of this tower.

Like *Alice in Wonderland*, the book she'd stolen as a child, at the farmer's market, when she'd wandered off from her mother's flower stand, allured as she was by a pile of used books, English classics. She'd rubbed her hands over Alice's shiny face, her blond curls around the blue ribbon she wore as a headband. She'd slipped the book in her apron pocket, certain she'd be sent to prison if she was caught. She never told Joanna about her crime, and now as she sprints to the next landing, up this vortex, Barbara doesn't know why she didn't confess her sin to her friend. After all, she was the only person who might have understood and forgiven her before Joanna left the community.

The men's voices rise up again. The jangling of keys, and then the beeping of an alarm. An engine starts and she ducks behind the nearest car. A few cars down, she sees a black station wagon like the one Mrs. Caldwell drove pull out. She holds her breath and silently recites the Lord's Prayer until she can be sure the car is gone.

At least there's a roof here, what God wishes for me, Barbara decides. *My stable, my cavern*, she prays. She is trembling less somehow, and then she thinks maybe she's getting used to this. Adaptation, the way of her people fleeing persecution for centuries. A few feet away there is a little patch of open concrete behind a pillar. The closest thing to bed she can imagine. She makes a pillow with her hands and lays down on the cold cement in the dark. She lays her shawl over her as a blanket and practices keeping still every time she hears another engine rumble nearby, every time she hears the men's voices on the level below, talking about the names of cars and jangling keys. She sleeps awake if she can call it that, her body resting, trying to rest, while her mind stays sharp. At one point, a rat skitters from under an adjacent car in the dark, its black eyes glowing.

She clenches her jaw and tries to pray again, but who would take mercy on her when she had no money to offer, no weapons to protect herself? She only has this moment, here, now, in the dark, as she rests her legs until morning.

When light pierces through the wide windows of the garage, adding a sheen to the tops of all the cars, she unfolds her city map, the one she made into a tiny square to fit into her palm. She unfolds

120

it and irons out any wrinkles around street names to orient herself. There is more beeping and engines starting below her, but she waits for silence, and then she begins to walk toward the stairwell as if she were just another driver who'd parked her car. Never mind she didn't drive or accept rides from strangers. No one had reason to question her, and she had no reason to tell anyone anything unless they asked.

Her ankles have resumed their trembling, but it's more out of fatigue and hunger than fear. Her eyes sting with the light passing through this window, this sharp, burning line that recalls hanging laundry at sunrise, when she's forgotten her sun bonnet. Her steps echo as she descends another flight of stairs, and then when she reaches the bottom floor, she sees the attendants, dressed as they are in all black with baseball caps. They have small badges pinned to their jackets as if they were policemen or security guards, but they aren't, she is certain. One of the men is staring at her as though she were a ghost, but he doesn't ask her where she's come from. He just turns back to the other man and hands him a set of keys. And then she passes the booth, no longer empty, as a car pulls up to the window, and an arm reaches out to pass a ticket.

She hurries past the booth and out into the sunlight. At least it isn't raining. At least she won't be cold. She walks quickly until she reaches the sidewalk, only to find a homeless woman, shoeless, on another street corner. The woman is holding a brown paper bag. She drinks from it and mutters to herself. She turns and looks at Barbara. "God Bless!" the woman says. The woman is missing a front tooth. Her hair is uncombed, her floral dress tattered by her ankles.

"God Bless," Barbara says, the first she's spoken since the corner grocery store. Her voice sounds quiet. Distant. She is as thirsty as the woman likely is, and she wishes she had enough change for a cold drink.

Why hadn't she packed a thermos? A piece of fruit? But as she's crossing the street, she feels a presence behind her, footsteps maybe. Was the woman following her? Did she want money from Barbara?

When she reaches the other side of the street, there is no one, just the same woman on the same street corner begging for change.

Barbara thinks it must be a sign, for just moments later she notices something silver beside a sewage grate. A quarter. She hurries to secure it. And then, as she continues to walk, keeping her eyes on the ground, she sees some other change like breadcrumbs. She gathers a nickel and four pennies.

Her knees throb. You've made it this far, she tells herself. Patiently, she keeps her eyes fixed along every sidewalk crevice, looking for more change. She isn't sure how much time passes before she finds a few more nickels, some dimes, but she takes what she's found to the small grocery store with the bullet-proof glass. Inside, the man behind the counter laughs at her, the same hard rasp in his voice. He is still laughing, this same sneer that will not leave his face.

"No Holiday Inn?" he says.

She is silent, wrists still trembling as she clutches the handful of change.

"What have you got?" the man says, still sneering. His teeth seem a darker yellow, his voice deeper. She's shaking as she places the change on the counter.

"Can I have quarters for this?" she asks.

"Short on your room bill?" he says. He is making a joke, an English joke, or is he mocking her? Does he think she's just a foolish Amish woman incapable of finding her way? Abraham once told her that the English often relied on sarcasm in business, and that you couldn't take it too personally, but something about the way he's still sneering—or at least seems to be—makes her wonder why sarcasm exists at all, if not as an excuse for a person to be mean.

She keeps her eyes on the countertop where the change is, enough for a bottle of water, but she won't buy it here. Won't give him that. Though all are equal in the Lord's eyes, how can she trust this man who continues to mock her? Silently, she waits for the man to hand

122

her the quarters she's owed. But now it's taking him longer to move about his register than it should. What if he refuses her the quarters? She cannot fight him or call the police. Cannot call home. *I am alone here*, the Lord reminds her. So in the way of the Lord she smiles at him, but she cannot help but think how false it is—in having spent her whole life believing her separateness would save her. In the end, wasn't she little more than a blade of grass awaiting the crush of an Englishman's shoe?

She closes her eyes while the man behind the register retrieves a pack of cigarettes for another customer in line, still denying her the quarters. How quickly he takes the money for the cigarettes, but yet he is still making her wait, testing her patience. She keeps her eyes closed another few moments, and when she opens them, she sees that the man has given her everything she is owed. She thanks him, yet he says nothing in return. He motions to another new customer ready to pay.

It isn't long when Barbara is on the street again that she sees the bright yellow sign for McDonalds. It almost glimmers at her in the sun, this promise of a bottle of water. But when she steps inside, she realizes she must use the bathroom first, as if the sudden possibility of a restroom has made her need to relieve herself unbearable. Did her daughter stop on her journey like this? Though she can't imagine the pain Emma must have felt pushing down on her. Seven months pregnant with Barbara's grandchild, she must have been gasping for breath that first day away from home, without a single person to call or help to the restroom.

She hopes no one notices her moving past the line to order toward a narrow hallway where there are signs for MEN and WOMEN. But when she reaches hers, there is a code to get in. She stares at the numbers on the box for a long time, until she hears a voice behind her. She jerks suddenly and turns around to find a woman there.

"The code's on your receipt," the woman says.

Barbara just looks at her, ashamed that she has no receipt to show for herself.

The woman seems to sense Barbara's discomfort. Maybe even her terror, the way her wrists and ankles will not stop trembling.

"Wait here," she says. "When my husband is out, I'll ask him for the numbers."

"Thank you," Barbara says. The code box flickers in the bright yellow hallway. Would God punish her for waiting here, failing to abide by English rules she never should have been tempting in the first place? But then the door opens, and the woman's husband comes out with the numbers.

"1-8-8-9," she says.

The light on the code box glints again, and she feels the woman's eyes on her waiting for her to punch them in.

"Do you want me to do it for you?" The woman says. Her husband is standing behind her, impatient it seems, to get on with where they are headed.

Barbara shakes her head forcefully. "No, it's all right, I can do it. You're so kind to help." Her own voice sounds distant to her, but at least the woman doesn't know this, doesn't know what to expect of an Amish woman lost. Estranged.

"Anytime," she says, and then she follows her husband down the hall, leaving Barbara alone again.

She closes her eyes and takes a long breath. When she opens them, she counts one, two, three and enters the code, but the door won't budge. She jiggles the handle a little, and then harder, surprised by her desperation. She takes another deep breath and tries again, and then a green light blinks. She's in.

Lemon cleaning chemicals fill her nose, commercial products she's never used. She looks down by her feet to ground herself while she uses the toilet, but these aren't even her shoes. They are Mrs. Caldwell's shoes, and for a moment it seems so absurd to be wearing the shoes of the woman who brought her here, the woman responsible for her daughter's leaving. Barbara is dizzy when she stands up and finds graffiti on the bathroom mirror she cannot bring herself to read, even as FUCK and HELL remain etched in her periphery. She hurries to wash her hands, and as she reaches for the machine to dry them, she sees her face in the mirror. Emma's eyes stare back instead of her own—Emma's child eyes—that night before bedtime when she asked if the book of martyrs took Beth the day the milkman came. For it was Beth who had sacrificed herself before the others.

Her breath turns short as she pushes the door again, stepping out into the bright hallway. It isn't too late, she decides. Never too late to play by the rules. She hurries to stand in line to order a bottle of water, but as she stands there, she can't help but notice the dollar menu. And her hunger the way it wants to compete with her thirst.

"Welcome to McDonald's, can I help you?" a voice says. A teenager, a young girl, in a yellow visor.

Barbara jolts. She hasn't finished reading everything on the menu. When she sees the option for a small hamburger, she orders it without thinking.

"Anything to drink?" The girl has dark eyes behind her glasses.

Barbara shakes her head. "No, just a burger please," she says.

The girl's hands move quickly on a screen, and then there's another screen that lights up behind her while another clerk shakes the oil from the fryer, the scent of it strange and specific at once, as if she'd been here before in an English dream.

She hands the clerk her dollar in change, and the clerk places her receipt on a tray on the counter. "Do you want extra ketchup or mustard?" The clerk is reaching somewhere below the counter, where all the condiments must be, and normally Barbara wouldn't ask for extra things, but she is hungry.

She nods.

"How many?" The clerk asks, holding a wad of small packets in her hands.

"Three or four," Barbara says without thinking.

And then her burger is ready, wrapped in more yellow, thin and crinkly under her fingers as she unfolds it in a booth by the window. Suddenly it feels like the greatest gift she's ever earned, the way a thread of steam rises up, and she smells all of the oils. She adds two packets of ketchup under the bun, her hands still quivering. When she takes the first bite, she is overcome by the salts mixed with the same stench of grease that filled the whole restaurant. The pickles mixed with the ketchup are her favorite part, so she adds more, some of it getting on her cheeks the next time she takes a bite.

She looks around, wondering if anyone has noticed. How could she be a real Amish woman devouring a hamburger in the morning? But the handful of English here seem too busy eating. The children who had been arguing are playing with their toys. She takes another few bites, wanting to slow down, but she can't. She finishes too quickly to feel full and wishes she had enough change to buy a soda, or a bottle of water that would travel well. There is a stack of empty cups by the soda machine, and she can't help but survey the options, just to see if it is something that might be worth scrounging more money for. And then she sees that there's an option for tap water.

At the Freez & Frizz, English water was always free from the machine, and maybe it's the same here. As she fills a medium sized cup with water, she can't help but feel God's eyes on her again. How many chances did she get to break the rules before it was too late, and there was no more salvation? Could she still call herself a good, Amish woman if she got away with breaking laws that were never hers to break? This world built on transactions that her people only ever allowed as long as it promised their survival. But where was the limit to this exchange? At what point did it become corrupt, unfounded and sinful?

Her hands shake over the cup as she drinks it by her booth. She cannot stop herself from drinking it all once she's begun, and when she finishes, she looks around. Wondering if the girl at the register saw her steal this water she didn't pay for? Or someone behind her in line who knows this water isn't hers to have?

But no one seems to notice her now, not even the man wearing a construction hat in another booth, this man who might have stood behind her in line. He's staring at his phone in between bites of his sandwich. Barbara breathes deeply. Air fills her lungs, her mouth no longer parched. Her stomach full. She has enough strength now—in this food, in this water—to continue walking until she finds what she's come looking for.

Girls Night

By Anthony D'Aries

"Is she ready?"

Jody looked like a new car—black dress and black shoes, gleaming silver necklace and silver earrings. She didn't take off her sunglasses. She held one hand over the bottom of her phone, the way Mark's mother used to do when she'd scold him for making too much noise.

"No, I know, I get it," she said, turning her back to him. "It's very sweet, J.F. But does a nine-year-old need a four-hundred-dollar electric guitar?"

Jody glanced back at Mark. He couldn't tell if she wanted a reaction or privacy. Mark looked at his hand, which was still propping open the screen door. Jody walked to the far end of the deck, one hand on her hip. Behind him, Sam's heels clacked against the kitchen tile.

Then she was on the deck, in a short yellow dress Mark had never seen before. She'd straightened her hair, sharp points cutting across her forehead. Her skin glowed the way it had when she was pregnant. She reached up to grab the zipper on the back of her dress. No stubble beneath her arms, no white balls of deodorant. Sam pulled her hair away from the nape of her neck and backed up toward Jody. Jody took off her sunglasses. She pressed the phone between her ear and shoulder, then slowly zipped Sam's dress.

"I don't know, J.F. Figure it out." Her phone beeped. "That dress is fucking *cute*."

Mark forced a smile. He felt like an old man at the park watching a teenage couple take pictures before prom. He almost asked Sam what time she'd be back.

"Have fun," Mark said. He leaned in. Sam offered him her cheek. He pressed his lips against it.

"Don't wait up, Mark," Jody said.

He shut the door and turned as if he had somewhere to be, something to do. But he just stood by the living room window, watching them slip behind tinted glass, and drive away.

—

Mark paced the house. He folded the throw blanket on the couch. He wiped the clean kitchen counter with a damp paper towel. Then he was in the hallway, in their doorway. They'd attempted to make the bedroom sexy, as they had at their apartment and the apartment before that. A red and yellow tapestry draped over the dresser. Two sconces holding unlit candles. A wooden full-length mirror turned slightly toward the bed. But eventually laundry and half-empty glasses of water and chap stick and cough drop wrappers ruined the vibe, made it look more like a squatter's cave than a sexy bedroom.

Mark rarely remembered his dreams. And when he did, they were so dull he never told anyone about them. You couldn't really call them dreams. "Replays" was a better word. He'd buy a black coffee and a buttered bagel from the café downtown and that night he'd dream he was buying a black coffee and a buttered bagel from the café downtown. No ex-girlfriends from high school or flying walruses, just boring Mark reliving his day. He'd wake up depressed, wondering: *is that the best my mind can do?*

But for the last two weeks, he'd had the same dream. He walks into a crowded bar with Sam. They approach a faceless woman. She reaches out and shakes his hand. Then she leans in and gives Sam a kiss, their tongues slipping over each other like raw meat. And that's it. Over and over and over.

He hadn't told Sam about the dream, but he'd wake up angry. He was short with her in the bathroom, the kitchen, wanting her to ask him what was wrong but having no idea what he'd say if she did. She seemed to interpret his mood as morning grumpiness. Or worse, she didn't notice at all.

What did it mean that the woman in the dream was faceless? Did it mean that this scenario was simply a half-formed fear, nothing to worry about? Or did it mean that the identity of the other woman didn't matter, that his wife would suck the tongue of any woman, at any bar? And the handshake beforehand. The confidence of that handshake. How Mark accepts the hand every time, lets the woman lift his up and down. How that up-down movement flips a switch, cements his feet to the floor, forces him to witness their kiss.

The books on Sam's nightstand, the podcasts in her phone were laced with words and phrases like "empowerment," "freedom from codependency" and "finding your path." She'd told Mark she was having an "awakening." Mark asked how long she'd been sleeping, but she didn't find that funny. Neither did he.

The women she listened to, the women she read, all survived horrific events. Rape. Addiction. Sudden death of a partner. The word "harrowing" appeared in several of the blurbs on the back covers. Mark flipped through one of the books like it was Sam's diary, her instruction manual. He read words like "identity" "self-actualization" and "gratitude." The authors were middle-aged. Strong women with sharp jawlines, weathered skin, deep eyes. One of them tried to cover her alcohol-damaged face with thick makeup. Another wore earrings of heavy red beads and black lipstick. Late at night, Mark imagined his wife barhopping with these women, laughing and dancing and throwing her arms around them. A familiar smile, a brightness in her eyes he wasn't sure he could coax from her anymore. She looked relieved to feel that expression again, as if her entire body had just exhaled.

Mark was giving her space. The implication being he always had space, that he roamed the landscape of their relationship like a bull. Recently, the news showed footage of a bull wandering the suburbs of Long Island. He'd escaped from a slaughterhouse. Just walked off the property, down the highway, and into town. He'd been trotting around culs-de-sac and across driveways for days. A big stupid animal on an island, thinking he's free.

—

"I always considered my wife to be reluctantly heterosexual."

Chris shrugged and took a bite of his tuna sandwich. He said it like he was sharing his preference for whole milk.

"What do you mean?" Mark asked.

"I mean, think about it, man. Most dudes are assholes. That's not news. You ask any woman to tell you a time they've been fucked over by a guy or hurt or worse, and they'll tell you a story. Multiple stories. You ask a guy the same question about women they'll tell you about an ex who didn't fuck enough or hated giving blowjobs or some other bullshit."

Mark bit into his sandwich and most of the meat and cheese slid to the back, leaving him with a mouthful of bread.

"I know it's kind of cliché," Chris said, "but if you were a woman, wouldn't you rather be with a woman than a man?"

"You're saying that because you're thinking like a man," Mark said, still chewing. "You're thinking you'd have the same brain but in a woman's body."

Chris nodded. "Maybe. I dunno. I just think you put a man next to a woman and most people, gay, straight, whatever, would pick the woman."

The bells above the café door jangled and a woman struggled in the doorway with a baby carrier. Some customers glanced up from their plates with indifference or disdain. An older waitress cocked her head and offered a tight-lipped smile as if to say: *It gets easier, hun.* Mark was the only one who got up and held the door open. The mother exhaled a "thank you," brushing past him to the booth in the corner.

Mark sat back down, half-listening to Chris. He thought of Marjorie. Sam said it was bad luck to talk about names too early, but even before she was pregnant, Mark knew it'd be a girl and the name played over and over in his head. Sometimes in the shower or while driving, he'd whisper the name, test it out. He liked the way the word felt in his mouth, the way it sounded like an ingredient in a soup. *Mar-jer-ree.*

"Anyway," Chris said. "How are things with Sam?"

"Ok," Mark said. "Same, I guess. Sometimes she looks at me like I'm not even a person. Like I'm a couch she wants to throw out but can't move on her own."

"Ellen gives me that look, too."

"Yeah, but Sam means it."

Chris nodded. "Are you guys going out tonight?"

"She is. Her and Jody are on their way to the city right now."

Chris raised his eyebrows and leaned back.

"Don't even say anything."

"I'm not. I'm not," Chris said. He thought for a moment. "I had to unfollow that woman on Instagram. Too much."

In Mark's opinion, Jody posted too often for a forty-seven-year-old woman. Mostly videos of herself in the kitchen or the garden, sharing a recipe for a watermelon margarita or tips on how to prune cilantro. But she also posted a lot of—Mark didn't know what they were called. Clips? Memes? Pictures of herself four years ago, overweight, in glasses and a gray sweatshirt: *How It Started.* Then a recent shot of her in a bikini, stretched out on a towel, her skin tan and tight, her phone at the end of her outstretched arm reflected in her sunglasses: *How It's Going.* During Pride Month, she posted a long paragraph announcing that she has, for the last several years, identified as bisexual and "stands in solidarity" with the LGBTQ community. She had close to seventeen-thousand followers, which Mark suspected was some sort of marketing scam connected to the make-up tutorials she posted from time to time. Sometimes in the middle of the night,

Mark would wake to Sam caught in the blue glow of her phone, her thumb hovering over an image of Jody.

Mark looked up at the muted TV in the corner. A reporter holding a microphone, standing in front of a line of trees, the headline below exclaiming: *Bull Still on Loose.*

—

Two years ago, Mark woke up, showered, got dressed, ate breakfast with Sam, placed his hand on her swollen belly, got in his car and headed to work. He followed his usual path, until he came to the first major intersection. Instead of making a left, he made a right. He took the on ramp, 84 West, and kept going. And going. And going. LAST EXIT BEFORE TOLL. He kept going.

He drove the entire day and into the night. Through three states. When he stopped for gas, he had trouble breathing, his heart throbbing in his throat, but when he got back in the car and kept driving, the feeling dissipated. He stuck his hand out the window, his fingers cutting through the wind.

He parked in the back of a mostly empty campground. For two days, he kept his cell phone off. He ate most meals from the hot dog truck up the road, pissed and shat in an old outhouse in the woods. The plan was to have no plan. To act on impulse. Something he'd never done in his entire life. Methodical. Practical. Those were the words people used to describe him. Reliable.

If someone asked him now "why'd you do it?" he wouldn't have an answer. Stressed. Overwhelmed. Fear of fatherhood. Mark latched onto easy answers. Quick responses he'd give to therapists for years. But honestly, for once in his life, he just wanted to do the wrong thing.

When he turned his cell phone back on, his voicemail was full. Dozens and dozens of text messages. His boss, Chris, but mostly Sam. The messages started out curious, then concerned, then frantic. *I'm ok*, he texted back. He hesitated for a moment, then added, *on my way home.*

Several hours later, he got a reply: *We're at the hospital. This is Jody.*

–

Mark turned down Chris's offer to grab beers. It was nearly dark by the time he got home, the late fall sky darkening earlier and earlier. The flood light flicked on as he pulled up to the garage. He shut the engine. The exhaust pipes ticked. The air grew warm. When the flood light went dark, Mark could see clear across his yard, to the tall brown weeds and wilted wild flowers at the edge of their property.

He checked his phone for any messages from Sam. Nothing. Then he checked Instagram. The first post he saw was a video of Jody at a rooftop bar. She held the phone over her head and turned slowly, scrunching her hair, scanning the crowd, the skyline beyond the floor-to-ceiling windows. Lights on the bridge in the distance draped like a necklace. Jody turned the phone a little more: the back of Sam's dress. A few strands of hair on the back of her neck slick with sweat. She was talking to someone but Mark couldn't see who. Jody leaned in and rested her head on Sam's shoulder.

The caption of the video was #girlsnight.

–

The first person Mark saw in the waiting room was Jody. She stood beside the vending machines, arms crossed. Dark circles below her red-rimmed eyes.

"How is she?" Mark asked.

Jody squinted. "Where the fuck were you? She's been freaking out for days. She thought you were dead."

Mark looked away.

"*How is she?*" Jody repeated in disbelief. "She's losing the baby."

134

Jody turned and took a seat at the far end of the waiting room. Mark stood there. He didn't think he could move unless someone told him, explained how. Then his legs went weak and he sat on the edge of the closest seat. How long did he sit like that? Finally, the doctors brought him and Jody into the room. Sam was sleeping. Her head slumped to one side. Mark and Jody stood on opposite sides of the bed. Jody held Sam's right hand. Mark held her left.

—

Mark stood on the deck in the dark. An image flashed in his head: Sam, pulling her hair to the side, exposing her neck, backing up toward Jody's waiting hands. Not his. Jody's. Sam hadn't even glanced at him. It was as if he wasn't an option. As if he couldn't be trusted with the simplest task.

The kitchen was quiet. He took a pint of ice cream from the freezer, sat on the couch, and turned on the TV. Grainy footage from someone's front door camera captured the bull trotting down the street. Big and slick and confident, as if it were taking a victory lap around the neighborhood. Different footage from a higher angle, maybe a security camera, showed him cutting across a strip mall parking lot. Now he looked smaller, lost, maybe scared. *This is day four of the bull's escape.* Some reports called it his "escape." Others his "rampage." Except for a garbage can or two, the bull hadn't destroyed anything.

The news cut to two men standing in their backyard, holding rifles. "That thing comes anywhere near my family and I'll shoot it dead."

—

Around midnight, Mark checked his phone. No messages. He lay in the middle of the bed, arms and legs spread like a starfish. Taking up the whole bed while Sam was out used to feel luxurious, taboo,

135

but now it frightened him. Nearly every night for fifteen years he slept next to her. What if last night was the last?

In the dark, his head felt like a lava lamp. Irrational thoughts, invented scenarios, hypothetical arguments and ultimatums oozed, contorted, folded in on themselves. How quickly little fears bloomed. Sam hadn't taken a night to herself in years. What was the harm? Let her go. Let her have her fun.

The dream returned. The anonymous woman. The handshake. The long, deep kiss. This time, Sam and the woman both wore red dresses. Mark had horns and stood on four legs, his front right hoof grinding into the floor.

—

In the morning, the clothes he slept in felt like a second skin. He checked his phone. A message from Jody: *Crashed in the city. Should be back later.*

Should be? What did that mean?

Mark rolled to the other side of the bed. The woman on the back cover of one of Sam's books—a German sex therapist who seemed to be everywhere these days—stared at him. Not at him—through him. She appeared slightly amused, slightly disgusted, as if he were a child interrupting a dinner party by running into the dining room with underwear on his head. The few times he'd heard her speak in video clips on the internet, he resented her all-knowing advice, the way she spoke as if every couple on the planet argued about the same things, in the same way, and really the solution was "quite simple." But what angered Mark the most was when she articulated an insecurity he thought was solely his own. How her words playfully tapped on his secret fears like a reflex hammer. "Yes?" she'd say after one of her observations. Even during her talks to large crowds, she seemed to be speaking directly to him. It occurred to Mark that everyone in the audience probably felt that way, which was why she was so successful. The illusion of intimacy.

The first few months after Sam came home from the hospital were the hardest months of Mark's life. She slept in the guest room and spent most of the day watching trashy reality shows, rich women yelling and crying. Mark brought her soup and sandwiches, water and tea, replacing empty dirty dishes with full ones. Some days, in the late afternoons, Sam sat in the sun in the backyard. Her head slightly tilted. Mark tried to sit with her, but each time she'd get up and walk back into the house. So, he left her alone and did the dishes, glancing at her from time to time.

Mark had read somewhere about people who survived a suicide attempt. They seemed to all have one thing in common: the moment after they jumped off the bridge or swallowed the pills, regret rushed through their bodies. Then later in the hospital, when they woke to friends and family surrounding their bed, the purest relief and gratitude pooled in their eyes. Many of the survivors described their attempt as a "turning point." But a deceivingly simple sentence half-way through the article revealed that this sense of relief and gratitude was not usually shared by the survivor's loved ones, especially their partners: "Husbands and wives of suicide survivors often have a much different interpretation of the event."

The second Mark stepped into the hospital and saw Jody standing in the waiting room, he was jolted back to his real life, the life he'd forgotten he'd wanted, the one he'd tried to run away from. And though he tried to explain to Sam that his impulsive act only reaffirmed his love for her and their life, he couldn't find the right words. Then the news that the baby—that Marjorie—was gone and Mark's cheap epiphany was irrelevant.

For the last two years, they co-existed. They'd go away for a weekend or have a long dinner at home and if the lighting was right, if they'd had enough wine, enough dessert, they'd slip into their former

137

selves and Mark felt close to her again. But it was a fragile spell, and by the time they lay in bed, they were like survivors of a shipwreck, floating apart on jagged pieces of wood.

Mark flipped Sam's book over and covered the therapist's photo. The hardwood floor was cold on his bare feet. In the kitchen, he stared at the backyard while the coffee pot ticked and gurgled. A thick mist had settled over the grass. The last of the dead wet leaves shellacked to the deck. He stepped outside. The closer he got to the mist, the farther away it seemed. He couldn't tell if he was in it or had moved through it. He reached the middle of the yard, turned around, and could no longer see the house.

—

It wasn't insane for a person to stay out all night with a friend. It wasn't insane for that person to spend the next morning with that friend. And it wasn't insane for them to spend a weekend or even a week together. Friends do that, Mark supposed. But Sam hadn't done it in a long, long time and she'd never done it with Jody.

Mark looked at Jody's text again. *Crashed in the city. Should be back later.*

Yes, Mark wanted to reply. You should be. But something told him they wouldn't be back. Maybe, at that very moment, they were Thelma-and-Louise'ing their way across the country. He couldn't remember much about the movie—just two women in their car, racing toward the Grand Canyon, a pack of armed men behind them.

Mark sipped his coffee. The mist in the yard had begun to burn off.

He turned on the small TV on the kitchen counter. Live aerial footage of a forest. A line of police cars and news vans at the tree line. BREAKING: BULL SURROUNDED.

One of the trucks at the edge of the forest wasn't a news van, but a cattle trailer. A man in jeans and a white t-shirt opened the rear gate. He held a rope in his hand, the other end tied around the neck of a cow. He led the cow down a short ramp, walked her through the line of police cars and out into the grass. The reporter said the cow's name was "Norma" and the plan was to use her to lure the bull out of the forest.

The man in the t-shirt backed away. Norma sniffed the air, then bent to the grass, took a large mouthful, lifted her head and chewed. She looked content. Bored.

"We'll just have to wait and see what happens," the reporter said. "The bull has plenty of food and shelter and fresh water in the forest, and experts say he could survive out there alone for quite some time."

The last shot was a close up of Norma's face, her back to the forest.

—

Jody's car breathed in the driveway. A warped and wavy image of the side of their house reflected in the black glass. They sat in the idling car for ten minutes, maybe more. Then Sam got out. Jeans and a sweatshirt Mark had seen Jody wear in one of her Instagram posts. Sam draped her yellow dress over her forearm. She bent into the car then stood straight and shut the door. Jody lingered in the driveway before backing out and pulling away, kicking a few pieces of gravel into the grass.

Mark opened the door. Sam seemed surprised to see him. They stared at each other. Neither one moved. Then he reached out to help with her bag and dress, but instead their hands met in an awkward handshake. In a dream, he'd lift her arm, twirl her like a flamenco dancer and they'd move in time, on instinct. But here, in the sharp sunlight, he just held on and waited for her to lead.

Medieval Death by Walmart

By Rachel Basch

I'd seen the costume on the kitchen table a few nights before, when Ben was at his mother's. A plush red and black, five pointed cap attached to a collar ringed with dangling skeletons. The mask was separate. Medieval Death in white rubber, by Walmart. Paul and I'd had a few drinks, and we took turns putting on the costume, looking in the mirror, scaring the cat.

I think about this now as Ben, who is 10, storms through the front door. It is Halloween night and also Paul's 51st birthday. Ben pushes past a group of trick or treaters, leaving his buddy, Rory, out on the front steps. I hadn't really wanted to try on the mask. Germs, for one, but, mostly I hadn't wanted to don "Scary Court Jester" because I knew it was the very thing Ben worried about when he was out of the house half of each week, my helping myself to what belonged to him.

"Hey, Ben," I say, as he blows past me, headed for the kitchen. "Can I take a picture of you and Rory." Paul hands me the mixing bowl filled with Twix and Three Musketeers, Almond Joys and M&M's and follows after Ben. I walk out to the front steps where there is a Mummy, a Vampire, a Lady Bug and two Hippies. I hold the bowl outstretched and comment on one aspect of each costume, the green eyes, the fangs, the wings, the flower-power head bands. Everyone over the age of four takes more than one of the mini candy bars, which I allow, though I know Paul wouldn't. During the six months we've been together, work has been slow, and Paul says if we play our cards right, we won't need to open the second jumbo bag of candy, and he can return it.

The front door is ajar, and from the kitchen I hear Ben hiss "she," not so much pronoun but curse. I hear Paul, too. "Because it's my birthday...to see you in your costume." Only one out of every 15 or 20 words is actually comprehensible to me, but the rhythm is unmistakeable. Ben's monologue escalates, a great pile up of language, rushing rapids on the approach to the waterfall. I can feel the crying before I hear it, a low rumble that runs along the floorboards from the kitchen to the the front steps. I shut the heavy oak door to give them privacy.

Rory and I stand outside between the two intricate Jack O'lanterns Paul has carved and which parents of trick or treaters have been admiring all evening. The bigger pumpkin has a pencil sticking out of it's forehead, a substitute for the steak knife Ben had first plunged there.

Rory is dressed in blue sweatpants and a blue sweatshirt. I have no idea what this costume is meant to signify, but he is still young enough for me to suspect that my confusion will be hurtful. I ask him if I can hold his bag of loot, to weigh the contents. He hands me the king-size, dark brown pillowcase, and I find it's both relatively empty and strangely heavy.

"How many houses have you gone to?" I say.

"Not that many."

I look inside the pillowcase and see a splint, a sling, a roll of gauze and two dirty ace bandages. "Someone handing out medical supplies?"

"I was supposed to be Broken Man, but no one got that it was a costume. People kept asking how I broke both my arms. Plus, all that stuff was bugging me."

From behind the shut door and the closed windows I can still hear Ben. I've raised two children myself, both grown now, so I know the lexicon of crying. There is that sound that babies make when they are hungry, tired, very hungry, very tired. There is the crying from fear, from frustration. Then as they get older, fury and righteous indignation. But this, this sound on the other side of the door, this is weeping. This is the sound of pure grief.

I ask Rory, who in the neighborhood is giving out the best candy? Who is handing out the worst? Which house is the scariest? Who has their lights turned off? He tells me that it's not the people in the biggest house who are giving out the best stuff. The Gorecki's are giving everyone full-size KitKats, but that's only because Mrs. Gorecki works for the company that makes them, and she gets them for free. The house with the falling apart stone wall in front, those people always turn their lights off on Halloween. And the house on the corner of Longview, where the grass gets really long in the summer, is scary even in the daytime when it's not Halloween.

After about 15 minutes of continuous crying coming from inside, I finally acknowledge it. "Did something happen?" I say, hoping against hope that something unravelled between kids, that one boy was mean to another, that Ben got left behind or left someone else behind, that some older kid jumped out of the shadows and scared the life out of him.

"No," Rory says. "Well," he pauses, his head now deep inside the pillowcase. He resurfaces with a bag of Skittles. "I don't know." He rips open the corner of the package with his teeth. "Maybe."

I nod. I wish this were only about candy, but I know Ben's crying has to do with me. Paul and I have been seeing each other since April, and we seemed to make it through most of the summer, before Ben decided that his father could not love us both. He's asked his father to stop calling me "honey," because that's what Paul calls him. He does not want me folding laundry or buying groceries. "You have legs, Dad, you can get us milk when we need it." When Paul calls me for advice while making pizza one night, Ben shouts in the background, "you never needed help making pizza before." After an outing to a local corn maze a few weeks ago, Ben broke down and told his father he was afraid Paul would love me more than him. Since then, I've made myself scarce when Ben is with Paul. I don't call, I wait for Paul to call me. I've stopped bringing over homemade cookies and little gifts of books or games I think Ben might like. Everything I do seems to cause him pain. The fact of me, no matter how studded with chocolate or festively wrapped, is a reminder that his life has changed again without his having been able to weigh in on that change. I only came over tonight after I was sure that Paul had okayed it with Ben.

Rory helps me hand out candy to the trick-or-treaters who arrive in spurts. It's begun to drizzle, and the baby in the lamb costume is a little matted. Hair dye runs down the forehead of the girl in the poodle skirt. I don't want anyone to hear the crying, anyone Ben might know, anyone who rides the school bus with him, so I make sure to talk loudly as the kids plunge their hands into the bowl full of candy.

In between trick-or-treaters, Broken Man sits down on the front steps, and I sit next to him. I wonder what I would do if he weren't here. About 90 percent of me wants to bolt, just get in the car and drive as far as I can from the sound on the other side of the door. Paul and I met by accident. Not one thing about the externals of our lives, not our occupations nor our backgrounds, is similar. No algorithm could have predicted that we would fall in love—precipitously, like teenagers, rather than people in our fifties, trailing the grief of failed marriages. Turn us inside out, though, and we are an emotionally matched set, as familiar to each other as to ourselves. I'd resorted to lame metaphors of magnetization to explain our fierce and fast connection. But now I am disoriented, temporarily demagnetized, sitting with a kid I don't know, holding a bowl that is not mine, filled with candy I did not choose, bearing witness to pain that I have caused, just by my presence.

When the front door finally opens, Ben pushes past us. He's not wearing his costume, but he has his pillowcase of candy slung over his shoulder. "Let's go," he yells back to Rory, as if Rory's the one who's been holding things up. They run down the front lawn and across the street. I go inside the house, where I find Paul lying on the living room floor in the dark.

143

"That was brutal," he says.

"What happened?"

"I can't stand to see him like this. It's literally breaking my heart to see him so sad. When he woke up this morning he told me Halloween was the greatest day of the whole year and..."

Even in the unlit room, I can see Paul's eyes, glassy and full. "It sounded, from outside...it sounded extreme."

"He kept asking why you were here. What you were doing here."

"You said you asked him beforehand if it was o.k."

"I did. He said he didn't want me going around with him this year, that I could stay behind and hand out candy and you could help me and..."

"And it is your birthday."

"When I told him you'd come to give me a gift, he screamed, 'I bet that's not all she's giving you.'"

"Whaaat?"

We laugh too loudly and for too long, a kind of crazed exhausted laugh.

"What did you say when he said that?"

"I said, 'Ben, what do you mean?' And he wailed, 'I... don't... know.'"

Paul's smile slowly straightens after he says this. "He got really upset about the card."

"Why?" I had purposely picked the birthday card for it's non-romantic nature. I'd bought it at the car wash a few days before. The cartoon on the front showed a dog peeing on a rug.

"'Why did she write Love on your card?!'"

"But I didn't," I say. I had thought this through, too. I'd simply printed a capital letter L followed by a comma. One letter. "Shit. I'm sorry," I say.

"You have nothing to be sorry about," he says.

I am at once suffused with annihilating guilt and an exquisite sense of injustice. I am a monster, hideously selfish, injurious to a child,

144

no less. Simultaneously, I believe myself to be the victim, terrifically misunderstood and as unfairly treated as Jane Eyre or Oliver Twist, an orphan in a loveless world.

"I'm sorry," I repeat. And I am, but not just for Ben.

With the story told, the reality of the situation returns. Paul stands, slumped in the hall, his eyes cast downward. I move towards him, and just as I bring my lips to his, he turns his head in the direction of the kitchen. "I bet you anything he comes through that door in 10 seconds." We do not kiss. Instead, he steps away from me, and the back door crashes open. Ben's in the kitchen, slamming his candy bag onto the table, Broken Man right behind him. Ben is short for his age and very thin, but he sweeps through the kitchen as if he were a multitude. He takes long, loud strides toward the refrigerator, grabs a juice box, jabs in the straw, like driving a stake into the heart of a vampire. He drags his bag of candy across the kitchen table, knocking Paul's new birthday wallet to the floor, then swings open the door to the finished basement, all 65 pounds of him leaping down the carpeted steps. Paul races after him, with Rory following behind.

I carry the candy bowl out to the front steps, though no one has rung the bell. I would like to remain even-keeled, unaffected, bemused, but I am caught in a love triangle, and there is no such thing as a love triangle without high drama or compromised integrity. I, too, am jealous. Though I have told Paul to tell Ben that love is a limitless resource, time and attention are not infinite. And just like Ben, I find myself not only wanting more of both from Paul, but believing that I need more. Ben and I are pitted now against one another, each of us operating from a conviction about the scarcity of love. I am horrified to find myself feeling like a 10-year old.

Four teenagers who have not even bothered to wear costumes, lope up the sloping, wet lawn toward the house. I remember the Halloween 10 years ago when my son, then 14, announced he was going trick-or-treating with friends. I told him that at his age, what

145

he was doing was tantamount to a hold up for candy. The kids who approach now are appropriately sheepish. The absence of costumes makes it tough for me to think of a single thing to say to them, but before they turn to go back to the street, the candy bars tumbling down into their sacks, I try to make out each hooded face. Is this one of the few instances in adolescence when kids wish they were younger rather than older, when they suffer the realization that some freedoms are lost, rather than gained, with age?

Back inside the house, I stand at the top of the basement stairs and listen to the video games and laughter below. I decide to descend. Paul is sitting on the floor with the boys, each one with a pyramid of candy piled in front of him. Paul sifts through Ben's pile and pulls out a Mounds bar. "Still hate coconut, right?"

"Hate's a strong word, Dad," Ben says, repeating something Paul is fond of saying.

"True," Paul says, pulling apart the wrapper on the mini candy bar.

"So, Ben," I venture, "What's your favorite out of everything you got?"

The boys are playing Minecraft, a little pile of discarded wrappers growing on either side of them.

I listen to the New Age soundtrack on the video game while Ben ignores me. I force myself to think about the music, the composer, the process. Did someone really write something so beautiful, incrementally, while watching frame after frame of this game?

"Laura asked you a question," Paul says after a long time with no response from Ben.

Ben is deaf and mute.

"What's your favorite, Rory?" I say.

"Sour Patch," he says, without looking away from the screen. "But if I don't eat the chocolate now, my dad will eat it all when I get home."

"Strategy's important," I say.

The doorbell rings. Paul stands and heads up the stairs.

"Are you going home soon?" Ben says to me.

"Ben!" Paul yells from the top of the basement steps. "Apologize."

"It's o.k.," I say. I laugh. "Actually, yes, I'm leaving momentarily."

"Why do you use big words? You do that a lot."

"Momentarily just means in a moment," I say.

"Dude," Ben says now, talking to Rory about the game on the screen.

I stand on the sea of beige carpet in the playroom knowing I have been dismissed and wanting to engineer a different end to this meeting. "What's the longest you've ever kept your Halloween candy?" I ask lamely. "When I was growing up my brother used to eat all his in about a week, and I would try to make mine last until spring. So, he'd spend six months trying to steal mine. It got ugly."

Ben does not answer or look up at me. But Rory says that his older sisters will take everything if his mother doesn't hide it.

I crouch down in front of Ben's large pile of unopened candy and sift through with one hand.

"Don't even think about it." He wheels his head around, finally making eye contact with me. His anger is breathtaking, and some part of me simply wants to study it, as if aspiring to grow into this kind of entitlement. But a much larger part is livid at his admonishment. I wouldn't have dreamt of speaking to an adult this way, no matter her transgression. I caution myself about the fight response rising in my chest. He has reduced me to a thoroughly unevolved combatant. His outrage has a kind of gravitational pull, and I am locked in its orbit. Were I not capable of a verbose inner monologue in this very moment, I might already be swinging. But I do not move. I remain balanced on the backs of my heels, and I smile. "That's one of the sad things about having kids who are all grown up. No one to steal candy from." I stand. I look down at his big pile of sweets. "Your dad's lucky," I say. I turn to go up the stairs. The soundtrack of the video game increases exponentially, and I picture Ben's little thumb, beating the hell out of the volume button.

I grab my jacket from the kitchen where Paul is cleaning up from the tacos he cooked the boys earlier in the evening. "Thank you for my gift," he says. "It was too generous. Really."

"You needed a new wallet."

"Only wish I had something to put in it," he says, reaching for a dish towel to dry the wet skillet in his hand.

"You will," I say.

"Someday, we'll look back on all this and laugh," he says.

I shrug, walk to the door, raise my hand to waive goodbye.

"What? You don't think we'll get past this? We just have to be patient, that's all." He looks to the open basement door, then blows me a kiss. "Text me so I know you got home okay."

I drive the 13 miles between our houses especially slowly, forcing myself to pay attention on the dark winding roads in front of me, rather than on the sad, twisty scene I just left behind. I hate driving on Halloween. I'm always afraid I'm going to hit a kid. I'm tired. Tired of problems. Tired of sorrow. Tired of worrying about children. I feel as if I've spent a lifetime worrying about children. I want someone to worry about me. Romantic love, early on, has us believing that it will make all things right, even our impoverished childhoods. Where there was dearth, now there will be plenty. Where there was darkness, now light. In the beginning, at the start, it's like a costume you get to put on, a mask that changes not only how you're seen, but more importantly, how you see. And then, just like that, the holiday is over, and you're back in your street clothes, an adult, whether you feel like one or not, and you remember that it's your job to do the care-taking.

Poetry

In the Gouffre de Padirac

By Laurel Peterson

Half lit and slick, stone floors
guide us along the underground river
by rock pools,
                        water collected
over thousands of years, dripped
into stalactites and stalagmites.

You and I follow the paths around,
            up the stairs and down,
taking photos in the half-lit dark
while I try to remember
to breathe.
            There's enough air
down here, I tell myself,
even if the lights go out

and we have to feel our way
in a long, sparkling line
of cell phone flashlights
back up
                        the five hundred
            slippery steps
to sunlight.

But it's more than satiny
limewater on stone
            or the press
of darkness that leaves me
                        unstable
in this alternate world.

We are losing the path,
                you and I,
as the future forms stone around us.

Beside My Mother, in the Canyon

By Shellie Harwood

I am eight, with my mother.
Her hair falls like a dark curtain between us
when she bends over me to tie the pack on.

We are in a canyon.
The quaking aspens stand sentry behind us
in a long line, rustling landscape into song.

What if I lose my way, I ask again.
She fingers the long petioles that cause the shiny
yellow leaves to lift and salute the autumn breeze.

She tells me to lie down in the dusty trail,
to stretch my limbs out wide and long.
She pulls a stalk from the aspen tree.

My mother traces an outline of me in the dirt.
She says, we're making a map of you.
Borders drawn, she lifts me carefully free,

so as not to disturb the boundaries, or the colonies
of crawlers trying to survive beneath.
We gaze long down on me.

She places a heart-shaped aspen leaf where the heart
should be, where the breeze makes it tremble,
rise and fall to a beat.

We gather twigs and vines for the veins and arteries.
When you are lost, she tells me, think of this canyon.
Return to the map of you, to the tapestry.

Where will you be? I ask her. Always somewhere close.
And she drops to the dust, guides me to take great care
to draw the map of her, alongside me.

Then we lie down under the guard of aspen,
each in our own land, hands clasped at the border,
so far from lost, so safe from singeing sugar maple flames.

And we wait long together,
as if night might come on like an undertaker
and pronounce our names.

Hal Loses Me

By Benjamin Grossberg

O monstrous! but one half-penny-worth of bread
to this intolerable deal of sack!

—*Henry IV, Part 1*

when he rifles through Falstaff's pockets,
finds receipts, and calls out to the crowd—

this the old man consumed in secret and now
we all get to know. Ha ha ha. But none of us

is safe, not even in our adorable jogging shorts
or pearl-gray button downs with white collars

that look, granted, spiffy. We all carry crumpled
in our pockets the receipts—the too-little bread

soaking up the wine we snuck into a corner,
the hidden pleasure or indulgence or weakness

(if that's what it is) unbalanced by Roman virtue.
Glance in the mirror more than is seemly.

Touch yourself, touch your partners. Touch
your iPhone, wallet, and belly button.

Run your palm amorously around the leather
of your new steering wheel. Run your palm

over your cat's silky back. All ten of your cats.
Go back to the fridge for another popsicle.

For a third, a fourth, a fifth. Watch an episode
past your bedtime. Then, since it's already

late, watch two more. The Hals of the world
lean with their torches into the long mouths

of the caves of our lives: always behind them
a stooping cohort of cacklers and goblin-kin.

They'll have every lineament exposed to light.
Let them. Stick your fingers too often, too deep

into any of the crevices of your body:
O the joy of a pinky investigating the inner

sanctum of the ear. Lawrence's phrase:
the inward of your you. Let your pinky palp

come upon its prizes and do not pull it out
even when you see him peer in the window:

Hal slumming it in his brown scamp drag.
And beside you on the couch, one of

the cats, back leg hiked up in inimitable
cat fashion, foot high above its head, toes

splayed in extasy as it licks bristled-tongue
clean all the territory around its anus.

Be that content. That brazen.

After Watching Film Clips of Calder and His Circus

By Gwen North Reiss

Knees on the floor, you placed the curved blocks
into a ring, settled your gravelly voice

into the ringmaster's grand gesture and tone,
and set them in motion—baroque urchins,

horses of looped wire, charioteers,
and tightrope walkers in hats and tails.

Louisa tended to the music,
though once, in a New York apartment,

Noguchi ran the Victrola.
Under raggedy coats and tutus,

spines curve, legs and arms
thin to precision. Hands are mittens

of wire. Tufts of yarn, thick and unkempt,
give the lion his mane and the clown

his oversized cloak. A stitched smile
cracks open on the trumpeter's

sock face. The elephant is all hoses
and block legs. The sword swallower's

mouth is a hovering O
at the hilt of the blade, and crumpling

under a jumble of beads, the exotic
dancer—tender and worn

out. Little dogs run
inside the wheels of the Pegasus

chariot. With puffs of breath,
cranks and turns, you engineered

bodies in the air. Later too,
what you made

turned, twirled, flipped, and flew.
In the workshop, a rivet

became an eye,
a coffee can

fanned out into the Medaglia
D'Oro wing of a long-legged bird

with a neck of Ballantine Ale.
Guerrero photographed the studio

from above—hammers and rasps,
a rain of steel, a bright

chaos, pools of light shattering
over all the gleaming metal.

Teardrops, paddles, and wings
carve a planetary arc through air.

Beasts crane upward
and stand their ground,

playfully unhinged from Earth. The sun,
through a big window, illuminates

your wild white hair. Lollipops
swing on their gallows.

The Stillness of Wild Things

By Jason Courtmanche

The road to the grist mill
splits into a Y
on the other side of the bridge
over the Fenton River.

Mid-July, the road and riverbank
are lined with Tiger Lilies.
The meadow grass is high
and Black-eyed Susans wave in the breeze.

A triangle of land is inscribed
by Chaffeeville Road where
it meets the two ends of the split,
and there sits a white house

where the caretakers live.
The wife feeds the wild life.
Orioles and tanagers, little brown birds,
squirrels, gophers all feed side-by-side.

There is a fox den in the woods.
The foxes feed, too, and have
grown bold around humans.
We have sightings of the adults.

This morning, walking my dogs,
we turned the corner from

Stone Mill onto Chaffeeville,
and I saw a flash of tail.

We rushed to the guard rail,
the dogs curious but calm.
I assume the animal long gone
but there sits beyond the rail

a small grey face, unafraid,
perhaps, but calm and still,
watching, waiting.
Maybe two feet separate

the noses of my dogs and
that of a small, grey fox.
One beat. Two beats. Three beats.
Still they stare. I tug on the leashes.

"Let's go, boys."
The dogs follow me.
The little fox turns his head
and watches as we walk away.

Pity

By Katherine Schneider

How could you hurt me? I have been so kind—
I winced and all my face said *take pity.*

I wove a quilt, I warmed you; you moved me,
took, but gave nothing, not even pity.

I have spent my life soft, speaking gently,
deferring, relying on your pity.

I have looked you in the eye—thou monsters,
who consumed me without thanks or pity.

There is no art, there is no subtlety
in the narcissist; he laughs at pity.

There is no shame, no self-effacing change
in the bully who reigns banning pity.

What kind of animal are these cruel ones,
so proud not to be kind or have pity?

From the time they met me, rejected me,
ridiculed and used me without pity.

And they will be the ones who seem to win;
and dazzled masses will forsake pity.

Worship a fatcat savior, slick and snide,
hate neighbors, deride the poor—no pity.

The beaten, sad Jesus said *love, mercy;*
they scoffed—*Man-up, I don't need your pity.*

There's no safe place here for a tender soul;
hold up your own light, don't expect pity.

empty nest

By Summer Tate

their small mouths
opened and closed like scissors

as moons came and disappeared
with the dawn

baby spoons tittered,
teetering on the edge of yesterday

their forked teenage tongues
squawked for freedom

fresh down feathers make home
worry the butcher's cleaver

will turn their chirping into battered wings
that tried too soon to fly

Bomb

By Joan Kwon Glass

In response to the arrest of Ahmed Mohamed in 2015

I guess anything can be mistaken
for something dangerous.
A child, for something sinister.
A clock, for a bomb.
A hedgehog, stripped of its quills,
or eyes removed and put back crooked
would be something unrecognizable,
something frightening.
I'll bet it took hours for Ahmed to take
that broken clock apart and fix it
at his kitchen table in Texas,
so proud he'd figured it out,
excited to show his classmates.
When his teacher mistook his clock
for a bomb and he was led away in handcuffs,
his quills fell off.
I wonder if they grew back crooked.
I wonder if they grew back at all.

Miscarriage

By Meghan Evans

Because it has been raining for days
even solid things like rocks
are fragile as sea sponges

The bark of our oak tree is pulp
foaming with steam and moss
sagging under strain of water

The dirt churns to mud soft as flesh
the way all humans become earth.
We all become earth, right?

I had been thinking of you
as a slippery leaf clasping its branch
with a stem-thin arm and knuckled fist

So when I dreamt of blood
wrapped around my legs like a skirt
the winds blew and you were   released

War, Again. Still

By Meghan Evans

This body is a survivor

It has a life of its own

The evening wind speaks to it

In her ancient voice

Let her tell of fresh blood

On your chin and the wail

Of your mother when she stopped

Counting the days of your life.

I am here

To listen. Listen

I bring the body of a woman

on the battlefield

My body   it belongs

Where the wet green earth becomes

history

Cut to pieces, laid to bed

Like a nightmare   my body

Is singing, this is how

Woman haunts

Always left

To make peace out of war,

To turn hatred into love

This body is a survivor

See? You will know   when

The rain is falling when

The curtains blow open

When every last soft joint is

covered in blood

Evensong

By Adrian Frandle

It's an elegant sycophant
    that skiomachy of ashcan
        and bongflicker on brick.
The wicker sweeper dangles and inverts
    the room with bristleskirt,
        its reeded plume. Fire not
in place, smokeless, consumes the cold
    surroundings, a ravishing absence
        of heat. Astonishment of ashes
that were never ours to bestow. Urned
    vase. If I'd wanted to take it all
        back, the whole room
           and totality of vision, evenso.

Alarmed

By Exodus Cooke

I found myself
when I opened death's casket
draped in my Sunday best
pale as death
painted a different shade
masked to hide
death's battle
etched on the face
of one who has lost
his life's fight
ahead of time
never took the time to pause
moved at the speed of light
flight of his fancy
do as he will
not missing a beat
yet missing life's
unique treats
beautiful memories shaped by
life's slow dance
with a moment
brief it may be
etched for an eternity
to be relived
in a moment of nostalgia
now just a
depressed nostalgic memory

imprinted on life's reel
time stamped
marking life's last dance
ending in
a brief abrupt moment
that mimics my time spent
in a blur
didn't see the signs
that read stop
nor the red lights
that warned me to stop
take stock of my life
for it's just
a wisp of smoke
lived for a brief moment
intertwined with life's tempo
a rhythm with which
I should have flowed
like a vapor's mist
dancing in tune with
nature's breeze
move at a leisurely speed
as it rises to pass
as if
it never existed
my existence
should have been
of equal measure
enjoying life's
sights and sounds
my surroundings
were full of life's treasures

no time to spare
to bask in life's
picturesque views
for my life wasn't
a timeshare
meant to be shared with
nor spent on
a passing moment
so I passed on
those life's moments
for time was
of the essence
no time to be wasted
on life's brief moments
that only took
a brief moment
to enjoy the moment
that I felt
took up too much time
now I find myself
face to face with death
dressed to the nines
not looking like myself
a sickly grayish hue
this truly can't be
I pinch myself
BEEP-BEEP BEEP-BEEP BEEP-BEEP
damn it's time
I pump my brakes
no need to rush
to an early grave.

Low Tide

By Margaret Sawyer

Down in dreams and tidal as
my window's view of sea marsh
whose slow-ebbing, on a bed like mine,
drifts soft with water
       and lifting grass.

One with the light wind's running
green through leaves and gold-shining
haloes of meadows, remembrance
goes rippling
       and wasting.

Old thoughts: a land song streaming,
unwinding, unwound, and all
its particulars just shadows
sliding slowly
       seaward.

And still they rise to frolic
so careless of all that:
duets of white butterflies
drawing up in their amorous
spirals the double helix
of small persistent dancing
that anchors
       the world.

King Ludwig II's Chamber of Mirrors

By Oliver Egger

Forty servants light two-thousand candles,
their light lonely in the midnight
hall, as their German king paces
his mirrored hall of infinite chandeliers.
In the morning, he will be dead,
his body bloated, drowned
beneath a mountain-laden lake.

Ludwig sleeps through the day,
wakes only with the moon, rising
in his half-finished castle dedicated
to the sun, the sun-king, his French hero
of the heavens, Louis XIV, whose black-haired
portraits hang between each lightless
curtain. He cannot be the sun
so he sulks in its shadow.

His chamber wall's gold tentacles
of glory are so unlike the tangles
of swallows beating in his ribs.
His chamber portraits of victory
raise their blades above his over-polished
crown. His chamber mirrors show
the outline of an imagined court,
flickering from the wicks of his empty
hall. Here bands should play and lovers
dance, their puffed-up dresses snatching

the silver moon, but alone now
he haunts his thousand slanted selves
in the chamber's reflection.

How Louis would laugh at him,
his sorry golden gown, his silent
court, the disgusting hole
of his speechless throat,
his enemies who can't see
the reason for these mirrors.

His enemies don't dance,
they don't watch their forms
between the candles;
they whisper in dusk dens,
they plan the pressure
of their hands as they hold
his breath beneath the cold.

The moon fades, the sun begins
to fill the reflection. In the forever
mirrors, the thousands of doomed kings
shed a few tears but wish they could sob,
weep with wonder as the sun-king
would—praising his palace,
his paradise, the unbearable
of that arriving dawn.

What I'd Tuck Under Your Pillow if I Could

By Lisa Meserole

for Divya

The sliver of moon I touched
       in the poem you encouraged me to share
and hung by the circulation desk
       for patrons to read. Yours was the light
I wanted to see when I checked out books,
       the day a waxing gibbous with you in it.

The same weekend of your death,
       but eleven years ago, a husband shot his wife too.
Her last act, to crawl to a safe place
       and call the police to save her daughter.
The next day a friend of mine married.
       I had to ask the police permission
to be in the neighborhood of the crime
       in order to see her put on her gown.
A portal of skylight wedded with her
       as she walked down the aisle,
but the main source of light was her.
       The radiance of brides on their chosen day,
never knowing what triggers
       the hands they join might pull.

Your son all grown up, running
              to call the police to try to save you.
    All the running, the crawling, the saving
                  of what we can keep.
The moonlight gratitude I'd slip
      under your pillow if I could.
The world needs more kindnesses,
              waning, without you in it.

Natives

By Carol Chaput

When gas hit four-fifty, they stopped mowing along the highway,
left only a three-foot wide strip next to the macadam. When
it went over five bucks even that strip happily leapt free,
hustling back into the bushes, rough shrubs, the wild trees, Quaker
Ladies in a drift so vast it looked like snow, then wild roses,
yellow hawkweed, blue iris and blue-eyed grasses, and pearly
everlasting, bower vine and boneset, all seeds ripening
once again, Queen Anne's lace, sweet nectar for bees and shelter for
insects, rabbits, the birds and turtles, milkweed, and Joe Pye weed,
starry asters robed in royal purple, shades of blue and pink,
and wild strawberries, the bright shadbush, blooming when the shad run.
When so much has been taken from us, remember it awaits
our return to wild fields, butterflies, the hay-scented sweet fern,
and right now, all those bees dancing in and out of goldenrod.

Ghost Apples

By Vivian C. Shipley

Like a robe in a closet keeping shape
of a body that wore it, crystal clear
shells of golden delicious dangle
from branches. Icing on contact, rain
has cocooned these apples, leaving
frozen skin clinging to trees.

Turning to mush before glassy shells
defrost, pulp oozes through creating
globes that haunt the tree. When I shake
them loose, the glassy shrouds shatter,
no flesh left to bruise—unlike my sister,
whose brain tumor rotted the stem
holding her body to this world.

Cremated, I buried her ashes
in the ground. Still unable to cry,
unshed tears freeze, dissolving
grief inside me that slips
away and melts into this earth.

Ode to My Digitaria (Crabgrass)

By Janet Krauss

Lavish yourself across

the wooden bucket, flourish

as you cover every inch

of the circle of cracked earth

that nourishes and helps you grow

on your stout stems into the hot air

and light where you flare out

like a dancer, finger-like leaves

velvet to the touch.

You defy the lack of rain

and you are the last of intense green

to remain until the autumn frost

finds you but maybe not

the small part of yourself

pushing forth from the crack

in the bottom of the bucket.

Burning

By Lionel Crawford

A pile of books, thoughts, writings
placed in a public place,
dowsed in gasoline and set ablaze.

Prefaces, dedications,
words left to interpretation
to nourish nations. Burned.

Truth and paper scorched,
torched to ashes, to dust,
the subjugation of the oppressed.

Suffocating smoke
of burning culture.
Charred remains of hope.

A pile of books, smoldering, embers
left in a public place
as unwritten intimidations.

Balaclava Weather

By Gaynell Meij

Mountain Laurel's leaf
green darkens to near black as
they roll in on themselves.

Nuthatch's white breast
feathers plump out, mimic
an icy snowball.

Behind glass, one black
cat stretches
to a lean line across the back
rim of the loveseat
absorbing all light and color.

Metamorphic rocks make no
apparent shift for cold.
Lichens hold firm. I believe
the moss would retreat
beneath oak roots if it could.

Layers of silk and wool
allow me to enjoy
the crisp and crunch, embraced
by cold clarity, I peel back
my balaclava to behold
my breath.

Generations Conspire for Us to Share a Green Juice in Central Park

By Christine Kandic Torres

Your ancestors
are not mine.

Arrowheads in the desert,
   canoes in the sea.
Earth versus water.
   Guano v. Hurakán.

Yet here we dance
beneath the new bloom of ancient trees
on the bedrock of an island
whose name remains unchanged.
Unlike ours,
long buried under swords and lisps,
a treasure map
inked in the blood
that rushes to your cheeks
when I kiss you.

Our tongues
fit lock and key.
An unburdening.

But which of us are prisoners,
I ask.
And which is the prison?

Disposition

By Mikayla Silkman

Everything is accounted for:
heart, liver, kidneys.
My mother's eyes tear up
as she reads each value—
an ounce, a gram, a pound.
My grandfather would have liked that—
everything itemized in an inch
of paper in a manila envelope.
My mother doesn't want my grandmother
to read it, and at first I do not understand,
until I imagine a faceless coroner
bent over his task, the dark weight
of each lung balanced carefully in hand.
I try not to think about the hollow ribcage,
the empty places where the eyes should be.
Instead, I imagine they've stuffed him
full of pages and pages of numbers,
and wonder how many ounces his life weighed.

The Thistle Bird and the Reaching Hart

By Devon Bohm

I have found the exact color of your irises, finally:
a winter's goldfinch shaking snow from the branches
with its weightless bones and brisk song, pitched high
so god can hear all its graceful hymns. Nothing is
hopeless in this world, everything is a gift. Take
the deer we saw near Penfield Beach just the other day.
No, I mean it. Take that image with you into the night's
real and definite darkness, held close and unequal
in your heart with fear: a fawn, really, making its way
over grassy hummocks with an unsteady gait to reach
the beans trellised in the neighboring yard. My irises
are the color of his new coat, newly born, and behind
them my brain is praying without ceasing and the prayer
is this: rich recitation, reverberating, hoping you can hear
that there's no virtue except to see what you can and
rejoice in it, my goldfinch-eyed blessing, my thorn-eater
of quick-flitting wing and song, each season, of praise.

Drought

By Elaine Zimmerman

Wrens line up in cracks for puddle water and seed.
Fewer wetlands, drought thins wing and flight.
Green boughs wait in heat and distance.
Streams stop flowing. Fish no longer cascade down.

Fewer wetlands, drought thins wing and flight.
Birds leave their nests. Eggs swept by wind.
Streams stop flowing. Fish no longer cascade down.
Who can protect when nothing endures?

Birds leave their nests. Eggs swept by wind.
The heart is often empty.
Who can protect when nothing endures?
Bugs and mice dig in to earth.

The heart is often empty.
Hungry for wing and wet.
Bugs and mice dig in to earth.
Even the horses lie down.

Hungry for wing and wet.
What was ripe is dry, hay piled up.
Even the horses lie down.
Sky vast with stars. Some fall fast.

What was ripe is dry, hay piled up.
There is little green beneath us.
Sky vast with stars. Some fall fast.
What's missing leads to thirst.

There is little green beneath us.
What's missing leads to thirst.
Wrens line up in cracks for puddle water and seed.
Sky, the new river, moves blue and fast.

Hunger

By Van Hartmann

Dark wings tipped like swords,
mocha-breasted swallows work the pond,
riding currents in graceful minuets
mere inches above the water,
swoop and dip to kiss the surface
in quick eruptions of silver spray,
their chests making brief contact,
then, returning to their element,
resume their dance across the sky,
but in that moment gleaning some morsel
from the feast-filled air, or the pond's wet skin,
their hunger fed by tiny-winged creatures
themselves scouring the plenty just below,
the porous line between worlds dissolving,
where the hunger ends, where it begins,
what hunger of my own this beauty feeds.

Walking With Wallace

By Heidi St. Jean

Inspired by the Wallace Stevens Walk, Hartford, CT.

Broken sidewalk cracks into afternoon
underfoot, we rise from the shade
and stand, still by Stanza II
the copper beech weeps around our feet.

Clouds feather themselves
into vertical wind-held quills, inking
the mythic wings of our involved lives
into the open papyrus of sky.

Circling, our voices at the edge,
we read as one, all thirteen
stanzas carved in stone—
I do not know which favorite to prefer.

We read, let silence cross at the green light
with the faintest flutter of shadow—
the blackbird lands, looks, throws us
the end-crumb of its backward glance.

Acknowledgements

This anthology would not have been possible without a generous anonymous grant obtained through the Hartford Foundation for Public Giving with help from Rough Edges Art Productions. Thank you to both of these outstanding organizations who make Connecticut a better place for the arts. Visit their websites for more information: The Hartford Foundation: www.hfpg.org/ and Rough Edges: reap1.org

About the Editors

Victoria Buitron

2023 Connecticut Literary Anthology **Editor Victoria Buitron** is an award-winning writer and editor who hails from Ecuador and resides in Connecticut. She received an MFA in Creative Writing from Fairfield University. Her work has appeared or is forthcoming in *The Normal School*, *SmokeLong en Español*, *Southwest Review*, *The Acentos Review*, and other literary magazines. Her debut memoir-in-essays, *A Body Across Two Hemispheres*, was the 2021 Fairfield Book Prize winner. A VONA fellow, her work has been selected for 2022's *Best Small Fictions* and *Wigleaf's Top 50*. In 2023, she received the *Artistic Excellence Award* from the Connecticut Office of the Arts. In June 2023, *A Body Across Two Hemispheres* won the gold prize in the Foreword Indies Multicultural category of Adult/Nonfiction. Her website is victoriabuitron.com.

Gates MacPherson

Assistant Editor Gates MacPherson was born and raised in Thorold, Canada, before migrating East to Massachusetts. She majored in English, concentrating on Literature and Language while competing for the Women's Track & Field team at Endicott College. She is currently producing her first novel of creative fiction, which she hopes to finish by the end of her undergraduate degree. Moving forward, she will return to Endicott to pursue a Master's in Business Administration.

Christopher Madden

Series Editor Christopher Madden is a writer, educator, and founder of Woodhall Press where he serves as the executive editor. He has a BA in English Literature from the University of Wisconsin, and an MFA in Fiction Writing from Fairfield University and an MFA in creative writing from Fairfield University. He is co-director of Bridgeport's Black Rock Arts Guild performing artists. He has edited numerous books including *Catchlight,* a Kirkus Best Book of 2020; *The Astronaut's Son*, a Foreword Indies winner for thriller/mystery; and *Light on Bone,* winner of the 2023 Maine Writers and Publishers Alliance literary award for crime fiction.

Contributors

M.K. Bailey

M. K. Bailey has a BA from Brown University and an MFA in Writing from Vermont College of Fine Arts. Her short stories have been published in many literary magazines including *Bellingham Review, Connecticut Review, Hunger Mountain, Confrontation, Gargoyle, Literal Latté* and *Slippery Elm Literary Journal*. She won the "New Voice in Fiction Award" from The Writer's Voice in NYC, and the Connecticut Film and Video Competition for *The Surgery*, a short film that she wrote, directed and edited. Bailey has received grants from New England Foundation for the Arts and Connecticut Commission of the Arts. She lives with her husband and son on an old farmstead in Connecticut and recently completed a speculative fiction novel *Just Start Screaming Now*. You can read more of her published stories at www.mkbaileyauthor.com.

Gina Barreca

Gina Barreca, PhD, Board of Trustees Distinguished Professor at the University of Connecticut, is author of ten books. These include the bestselling *They Used to Call Me Snow White, But I Drifted* as well as *Babes in Boyland: A Personal History of Co-Education in the Ivy League,* and *It's Not That I'm Bitter...: Or How I Learned to Stop Worrying About Visible Panty Lines and Conquered the World.* Her books have been translated into Chinese, Japanese, German, Portuguese, and Spanish and she's recognized internationally as an expert on gender and humor. Called "Smart and funny," by *People* magazine and deemed a "feminist humor maven" by *Ms.* magazine, Barreca has been published by *The New York Times, The Independent of London, The Chicago Tribune, The Washington Post, Cosmopolitan, The Harvard Business Review*, and appeared, often as a repeat guest, on the *Today* show, CNN, the BBC, PBS, NPR, and 20/20. Gina's *Psychology Today* blog has received more than 7.5 million views. She's editor of the *Fast Women* series for Woodhall Press, and can be found in the Library of Congress or the make-up aisle at Walgreens.

Rachel Basch

Rachel Basch is the author of three novels: *The Listener* (Pegasus Books), short listed for The 2016 Firecracker Awards by the Community of Literary Magazines and Presses, *The Passion of Reverend Nash* (W.W. Norton), named one of the five best novels of 2003 by *The Christian Science Monitor*, and *Degrees of Love* (W.W. Norton, Harper Paperbacks), a selection of *The Hartford Courant's* Book Club. Basch has reviewed books for *The Washington Post Book World*, and her nonfiction has appeared in n+1, *Salon, The Huffington Post, The Millions* and *Literary Hub*. In 2020, The North Shore Readers Theater presented her full-length play, *How-To.* Basch was a 2011 MacDowell Colony Fellow. She teaches in the MFA Program at Fairfield University and lives in Newtown, CT.

Michael Belanger

Michael Belanger is an author and high school history teacher. His debut novel, *The History of Jane Doe*, was a finalist for the Connecticut Book Award and received a *Kirkus* starred review. More recently, his writing has appeared in *Flash Fiction Magazine* and *Pigeon Review*. In addition to teaching and writing, he serves as a faculty advisor to *Greenwitch*, a high school literary magazine that has published talented young writers—including Truman Capote—for over a hundred years. His novel *Grimwell* won the 2023 Fairfield Book Prize and will be published in 2024. He lives in Connecticut with his wife, son, and two wonderfully aloof cats.

Chris Belden

Chris Belden is the author of the novels *Carry-on* and *Shriver* (adapted into the film *A Little White Lie*) as well as the story collection *The Floating Lady of Lake Tawaba*. He is also editor of *Closer to Freedom: Prose & Poetry from Maximum Security*, a collection of work from the prison writing workshop he ran for ten years. A 2019 Connecticut Art Hero and graduate of the Fairfield University MFA program, Chris leads workshops at the Westport Writers Workshop and cohosts (with Katherine Schneider) the livestream reading series "FUMFA Poets & Writers Live." Chris Belden's story, *Trust Fall*, originally appeared in *The Under Review*.

Devon Bohm

Devon Bohm received her BA from Smith College and earned her MFA with a dual concentration in Poetry and Fiction from Fairfield University. She has been awarded the Hatfield Prize for Best Short Story, was longlisted for *Wigleaf*'s Top Very Short Fictions, and has received two honorable mentions in L. Ron Hubbard Writers of the Future Contest—winning the contest in the 2nd Quarter of 2022. Her work has also been featured in publications such as *Labrys*, *The Graveyard Zine*, *Horse Egg Literary*, *Necessary Fiction*, *Eunoia Review*, *Spry*, *Sixfold*, *Hole In The Head Review*, *orangepeel*, *Helix Magazine*, *boats against the current*, Sunday Mornings at the River's *365 Days of Covid* anthology, and *Discretionary Love*. Her first book of poetry, *Careful Cartography*, was published in November 2021 by Cornerstone Press as part of their Portage Poetry series. The collection was the recipient of the 2022 First Horizons Book Award and was shortlisted for the 2022 Eric Hoffer Award, receiving the distinction for an outstanding publication by an academic press. Follow her on Instagram or TikTok @devonpoem or visit her website at www.devonbohm.com.

Carol Chaput

Carol Chaput's poems have recently appeared in Grayson Books, *Waking Up to the Earth, Connecticut Poets in a Time of Global Climate Crisis.* I was the recipient of the 2020 Nutmeg Poetry Award from The Connecticut Poetry Society. A collection of my poems, *Field Notes*, was published by *Dogwood Press*, and my work has appeared in poetry collections, including *Potpourri, Calliope, The Red Fox Review, Earth Day Poems* (CT-DEP), and *Stray Branch*. A long-time environmental and peace activist, human rights, climate justice, and social concerns strongly influence my work. You can visit my website at www.carolchaput.com.

Gabi Coatsworth

Gabi Coatsworth was born in Britain, but has spent most of her life trying to figure out how America works by living here. So, if you find a British flavor in her books, don't be surprised. She's an award-winning writer, who's had short stories and essays published in journals and anthologies, and her memoir, *Love's Journey Home*, published in 2022 by Atmosphere Press, reached number 1 on the Amazon new releases charts. Her debut novel, *A Beginner's Guide to Starting Over*, came out in April 2023. She is active in the Connecticut writing community and runs several groups for writers, including a monthly open mic Meetup, a monthly Writers Rendezvous, and a weekly write-in. If she's not writing or traveling, she'll be in her flower garden, wondering whether to weed, or relaxing with a book. Find out more about her at gabicoatsworth.com.

Michael Todd Cohen

Michael Todd Cohen's work appears in *Catapult, Columbia Journal,* and *Pithead Chapel,* among others. His writing has been nominated for a Pushcart Prize. He lives with his husband and two dogs by a rusty lighthouse in Connecticut. Read more of his work at michaeltoddcohen.com.

Exodus Cooke

Exodus Cooke was born in Bridgeport, Connecticut. Since his incarceration, he's tutored prisoners on their GED and worked with prisoners having mental health issues. As a Christian man he's also a member of the Kairos community. When Exodus was younger, teachers and mentors told him he should write. Having no confidence, he didn't take his writing seriously until 2014. He's had poetry and short stories published in three books with several poems printed in a magazine. At present he's putting the final touches on his book titled: *To Him*, a compilation of poems placing the woman on a pedestal and the man on the throne.

Jason Courtmanche

Jason Courtmanche is Associate Professor in Residence in English, Affiliate Faculty in Teacher Education, Director of the Connecticut Writing Project, and Assistant Coordinator of Early College Experience English at UConn. Recent publications have appeared in *English Journal, CT Literary Anthology, MLA Professions, WPA: Writing Program Administration,* and *Deep Reading,* volumes 1 and 2. He has won several teaching awards, including UConn's 2021 Honors Faculty Member of the Year and 2022 Faculty Excellence in Undergraduate Teaching.

Lionel M. Crawford

Lionel M. Crawford is a multi-faceted creative who enjoys exploring music, art, and writing. Lionel has been a musician since his early teens, composing lyrics and music in several music genres, including R&B and Soca. As a visual artist (oils, pencil) he has exhibited at The Joseloff Gallery, Hartford Art School, University of Hartford, C.R.T Craftery, Hartford, CT and the Queen's Park Gallery, Barbados. As a writer, Lionel has always written poetry and lyrics. His poem "Alexander (Calder)" was first published in *Fraud* (University of Hartford). "Learning To Feel The Rhythm," a dedication to Cheryl Smith's dance class, was included in The Artists Collective, Inc., Student Festival Booklet '96. He combines poetry with his musical compositions to create poetic pieces. Lionel is a graduate of Hartford Art School, University of Hartford, where he received his BFA.

Anthony D'Aries

Anthony D'Aries is the author of *The Language of Men: A Memoir* (Hudson Whitman Press, 2012), which received the PEN Discovery Prize and Foreword's Memoir-of-the-Year Award. His work has appeared in *McSweeney's, Boston Magazine, Solstice, Shelf Awareness, The*

Literary Review, Memoir Magazine, Sport Literate, Flash Fiction Magazine, and elsewhere. He currently directs the low-residency MFA in Creative and Professional Writing at Western Connecticut State University. His story, *Girls Night,* originally appeared in *South 85.*

Oliver Egger

Oliver Egger is a poet born and raised in Durham, North Carolina. He is a senior at Wesleyan University studying English and Religion who founded The Route 9 Literary Collective (route9.org), an organization supporting writers at Wesleyan and in the Middlesex County community. He edited and compiled a literary anthology entitled *The Route 9 Anthology: A Collection of Writing from Wesleyan University Students, Faculty, Staff, & Middlesex County Residents* which was published in Fall 2022 by Wesleyan University Press. His poetry can be found in *The California Quarterly, Oyster River Pages, Moonstone Press,* and more. In addition, he was named a 2023 Connecticut Student Poet by the Connecticut Poetry Circuit.

Meghan Evans

Meghan Evans is a Connecticut native. She earned her MFA in writing from Sarah Lawrence College. She is a Prose Editor for *3Elements Review* and teaches Literature at Central Connecticut State University. When she isn't reading student papers she's still reading something, somewhere.

196

Suzanne Farrell Smith

Suzanne Farrell Smith is the author of three books: *The Memory Sessions*, a memoir about searching for lost childhood memory; *The Writing Shop*, a teaching guidebook; and *Small Off Things: Meditations from an Anxious Mind*, an essay collection. She is widely published, has been Notable in *Best American*, and won a Pushcart. Suzanne teaches at Westport Writers' Workshop and publishes *Waterwheel Review*. She lives in a creek-cut valley in Connecticut with her husband and three sons.

Adrian Frandle

Adrian Dallas Frandle (they/he) is a queer fish who writes poems to and for the world about its future. They are Poetry Acquisitions Editor for *Variant Lit Mag/ Press* and MFA candidate at Randolph College. BOTN '22 Nominee. When not writing, you will find them walking their pair of chihuahuas near the lighthouse. More work online at adriandallas.com, on Twitter @adrianf & Instagram @afrandle

Jaclyn Gilbert

Jaclyn Gilbert is the author of *Late Air*, published by Little A in 2018. She holds an MFA in Fiction from Sarah Lawrence College, was a 2019 artist in residence at the Byrdcliffe Colony in Woodstock, and her short fiction, essays, and book reviews have appeared in *Post Road Magazine, Tin House, Lit Hub, Paper Brigade*, and elsewhere. Most recently, she founded Drift(less) Literary as an agenting collective to support writers of genre-defying work in partnership with independent presses based locally and abroad.

Benjamin Grossberg

Benjamin S. Grossberg's latest book, *My Husband Would* (University of Tampa, 2020), won the 2021 Connecticut Book Award. His other books include *Space Traveler* (University of Tampa, 2014) and *Sweet Core Orchard* (University of Tampa, 2009), winner of the Lambda Literary Award. He is Director of Creative Writing at the University of Hartford.

Van Hartmann

Van Hartmann taught English at Manhattanville College for over forty years. I've published two books of poems, *Shiva Dancing* (2007) and *Riptide* (2016), and a chapbook, *Between What Is and What Is Not* (2010). Individual poems have appeared in a variety of literary journals. I live in Norwalk, Connecticut with my wife, fellow teacher and writer, Laurel Peterson, along with our frisbee loving labrador retriever, Calder.

Shellie Harwood

Shellie Harwood is a Connecticut poet, actress, and playwright. Her poetry has appeared in *Tulip Tree Review*, *Oberon*, *Mudfish22*, *Connecticut River Review* and *Sixfold Poetry*. She won the 2022 Nutmeg Poetry Award for her poem, *Afterswarm*; also, 2nd Prize, Connecticut Poetry Award, 2022, for *What Bloomed in Dresden*. Shellie's chapbook, *With My Sister, in a Tornado Warning*, was published by Finishing Line Press (2021). The title poem was awarded the 2021 Oberon Herbert Poetry Prize. Her chapbook, *Sleepwalker's Guide to Grieving*, will be published in 2023. Shellie's poem *Nocturne 20/ Away to Nowhere* was a finalist for the 2022 Montreal International Poetry Prize and is published in the 2022 Montreal Poetry Prize Anthology.

Michelle Hernandez

Michelle Hernandez is a Dominican-American writer born and raised in the Bronx. She obtained her Masters of Fine Arts in Creative Writing with a concentration in Poetry and Non-Fiction. Michelle writes nonfiction and poetry as a form of activism and social justice to inform readers regarding underrepresented communities and overlooked realities. She aspires to have her first memoir, a collection of essays on class, ethnicity, education, and feminism, published soon. She is dedicated to educating and empowering society by using her writing to share her experiences with the world. To read her published works and get in contact with her, please visit writermichellehernandez.com.

Elizabeth Hilts

Elizabeth Hilts was born in Michigan but was relocated to Connecticut by the time she was six months old; other than a few forays to other states (only one of which was her choice), she has lived in the Constitution State ever since. The author of *Getting in Touch With Your Inner Bitch* (Sourcebooks) and *Every Freaking! Day with Rachell Ray: An Unauthorized Parody* (Hachette/Grand Central Publishing), Hilts has an MFA in Creative Writing from Fairfield University.

Sonya Huber

Sonya Huber is the author of eight books, including the forthcoming *Love & Industry* from Belt Publications, the new guide, *Voice First: A Writer's Manifesto*; and the award-winning essay collection on chronic pain, *Pain Woman Takes Your Keys and Other Essays from a Nervous System*. Her other books include *Supremely Tiny Acts: A Memoir in a Day, Opa Nobody, Cover Me: A Health Insurance Memoir*, and *The Backwards Research Guide for Writers*. Her work has appeared in the *New York Times, Brevity, Creative Nonfiction*, and other outlets. She teaches at Fairfield University and in the Fairfield low-residency MFA Program.

Vesna Jaksic Lowe

Vesna Jaksic Lowe is a freelance writer and communications consultant. She runs a monthly newsletter, *Immigrant Strong*, which focuses on writing by immigrants and children of immigrants. Vesna, who grew up in the former Yugoslavia, has written about her immigrant experience for *The New York Times*, *The Washington Post*, *Catapult*, *Pigeon Pages*, and the *New York Daily News*, and taught workshops on writing about immigrant life for Cooper Street Writing Workshops. She participated in the 2021 Martha's Vineyard Institute of Creative Writing's conference as a first-prize parent-fellow and the 2021 Tin House Summer Workshop. As a communications consultant, she works for nonprofits in the human rights and social justice space, and has completed projects for organizations such as the Brennan Center for Justice, the Inter-Parliamentary Union, PEN America, and Watchlist on Children and Armed Conflict. Find her on twitter (https://twitter.com/vesnajaksic), instagram (https://www.instagram.com/vesnajaksiclowe/) or her website (http://vesnajaksic.com/), or subscribe to her free monthly newsletter at https://immigrantstrong.substack.com/.

Christine Kalafus

Her essays have appeared in *Longreads*, *PAGE*, *The Writer in the World*, and *The Woven Tale Press*. "Horses," selected by Mark Doty as the winner of the Knightville Poetry Award, appeared in *The New Guard* and was nominated for a Pushcart Prize. Her unpublished manuscript

Blueprint for Daylight, a memoir of infidelity, cancer, colicky twins, and the flood in her basement, was excerpted in *Connecticut's Emerging Writers*. Current projects include shopping a debut poetry collection, polishing her first novel, and editing *Get Lit Barbie*, an invitational zine. Christine facilitates the community program Quiet Corner Poets and is poet laureate of Pomfret, Connecticut.

Christine Kandic Torres

Born and raised in New York City, Christine Kandic Torres is a writer with Puerto Rican and Croatian roots. She is the author of the debut novel, *The Girls in Queens* (HarperVia, 2022). Her Pushcart Prize-nominated short fiction has been published in *Catapult, Kweli, The Offing, Fractured Lit, and Lunch Ticket,* amongst others. She currently lives in Connecticut with her family.

Janet Krauss

Janet Krauss, after retirement from teaching English at Fairfield University, continues to mentor students, lead a poetry discussion at the Wilton Library, participate in a CT Poetry Society Workshop and two poetry groups. With Christopher Madden, she co-leads the Poetry Program of the Black Rock Art Guild. She has two books of poetry: *Borrowed Scenery* (Yuganta Press) and *Through the Trees of Autumn* (Spartina Press).

Joan Kwon Glass

Joan Kwon Glass is the Korean American author of *Night Swim* (Diode Editions, 2022) and three chapbooks including *If Rust Can Grow On The Moon* (Milk & Cake Press, 2022). She serves as poet laureate for Milford, CT, as Editor in Chief for *Harbor Review* and as a Brooklyn Poets mentor. Her work has won or been nominated for prizes such as the Pushcart Prize, Sundress Best of the Net, the Washburn Prize, Subnivean Award and Lumiere Review Award. Joan's poems have been published in or are forthcoming in *Prairie Schooner*, *Asian American Writer's Workshop*, *Rattle*, *RHINO*, *Dialogist* and elsewhere. Her featured poem, *Bomb*, originally appeared in *Porcupine Literary*.

Eden Marchese

Eden Marchese is an undergraduate at Fairfield University where they have been awarded the Nicolas M. Rinaldi Fiction Award for 2020 as well as 2021 in addition to the 2021 English Award for nonfiction. In their time at Fairfield, they have been devoted to developing their writing through their major in English: Creative Writing as well as Philosophy as they aim to create stories that connect with those who have felt voiceless. In xyr's development of their writing, xyr has been devoted to creating short stories that range from poetic, to gruesome, to holy and have used this range in xyr work on a book series titled the "Forsaken Genesis Duology."

Rowan Marci

Rowan Marci is an author of speculative fiction. She draws inspiration from the complex and beautiful experiences of being disabled, queer, and human. When not writing, Rowan works as a mental health provider for youth. Her short stories have been published in anthologies by *Quillkeepers Press* and Northern Connecticut Writers Workshop. She lives in northwest Connecticut with her partner, two kids, and too many pets.

Liz Matthews

Liz Matthews holds a Master of Fine Arts in Writing from Vermont College of Fine Arts. She is the Program Director of the Westport Writers' Workshop, a nonprofit literary organization based in Westport, CT, where she also teaches fiction workshops. Her short fiction and essays have appeared *The Tishman Review, Brain Child, The Rumpus, Big Fiction Little Truths*, and *Five South*, among other places. She lives in Fairfield with her husband and two children.

Gaynell Meij

Gaynell Meij has been a geologist, has become a naturalist, a tactile artist, and has been opened up along the way by deep ecologists and mystics. She has traveled the path of rational-analytic mind to sensuous matter and is now immersed in the blending of these ways. She is blessed to have a daily life that includes stillness and opportunities to observe and wander and give creative expression to inner and outer landscapes. Giving voice to ecologic realities in metaphor and archetypal stories at open mic readings is one form of her creative resistance to the denigration of the sacred.

Lisa Meserole

Lisa Meserole teaches music and movement to young children in Connecticut. Her poems have appeared in *Waking Up to the Earth: Connecticut Poets in a Time of Global Climate Crisis,* and in *Oysterville: Poems,* as well as in journals such as *Connecticut River Review, Green Hills Literary Lantern,* and *Shot Glass Journal.* She was an Edwin Way Teale Writer-in-Residence at Trail Wood, a program sponsored by the Connecticut Audubon Society.

Laurel S. Peterson

Laurel S. Peterson is a community college English professor whose poetry has been published in many literary journals. She has two poetry chapbooks, *That's the Way the Music Sounds* (Finishing Line) and *Talking to the Mirror* (Last Automat), and two full-length collections, *Do You Expect Your Art to Answer?* and *Daughter of Sky* (Futurecycle). She has also written two mystery novels, *Shadow Notes* and *The Fallen* (Woodhall Press). She is on the editorial board of *Inkwell* magazine and the Norwalk Public Library Board and served as Norwalk, Connecticut's Poet Laureate from April 2016 – April 2019.

Gwen North Reiss

Gwen North Reiss has published poems in *Rhino, In Print, Connecticut Review, Mom Egg Review, Dogwood,* and other literary magazines. She is the author of a chapbook, *Notes on Metals,* and *Paper Aperture,* a group of poems published by Pen and Brush in New York as an e-publication. Her poem, "Illuminated," was the winner of the Rachel Wetzsteon Prize at the 92nd Street Y's Unterberg Poetry Center. Reiss has a degree in Literature from Yale and began her career in book publishing before becoming a full-time writer. She has studied poetry at the 92nd Street Y, the Westport Writers Workshop, and Sharon Dolin's workshop program in Barcelona on ekphrastic poetry. She also writes about contemporary art and modern architecture and is co-author, with Alan Goldberg, of *Oaxacan Folk Art: Response to Covid-19*, published in 2021 by the Mexican Museum in San Francisco.

Bessy Reyna

Born in Cuba and raised in Panama, she is an award-winning writer whose work has appeared in numerous anthologies and literary magazines in the USA and Latin America. The author of *Ab Ovo*, short stories in Spanish, and the poetry chapbooks *She Remembers*; *The Battlefield of Your Body* and *Memoirs of the Unfaithful Lover/Memorias de la amante infiel*. Reyna was selected as Latina Citizen of the Year by the State of CT Latino/Puerto Rican Affairs Commission and is a recipient of a Lifetime Achievement Award by the CT Center for the Book, an affiliate of the Library of Congress for her work in support of literature in CT. (bessyreyna.com)

David Ryan

David Ryan's fiction is forthcoming or recently appears in the *O. Henry Prize Stories*, *Harvard Review*, *Georgia Review*, *Copper Nickel*, *Fence*, *The New England Review*, *The Common*, *The Threepenny Review*, *Conjunctions*, *New Letters*, and elsewhere. A recent recipient of an Artistic Excellence fellowship from the Connecticut Office of the Arts, he is the author of *Animals in Motion: Stories* (Roundabout Press). His story, *Your Silent Face*, was originally published under a separate title in *North American Review*. There's more about him at www.davidwryan.com.

Margaret Sawyer

Margaret Sawyer is a CT grandmother and photojournalist, who after forty years of international living, writing and exhibiting returned to her Darien hometown to continue doing more of the same. After leaving her features' editor job at her local newspaper, *The Darien Times*, she moved to East Haven to teach Visual Arts in a New Haven magnet high school. Her photography book of those years, *City School*, will be out in February. Simultaneously, she has continued her interest in poetry since first teaching creative writing at a community college in the Philippines under a USAID grant in 1970. Concurrently, she remains active with and a contributor to the anthologies of *Caduceus* and the Guilford Poets Guild.

Katherine Schneider

Katherine Schneider is a poet living in Norwalk, CT. She holds an MFA from Fairfield University's low residency MFA program where she worked closely with Baron Wormser and the late Dr. Kim Bridgford. She has also received an MA in TESOL and has taught ESL to adult students in the greater NYC area for 10 years. Being an active participant in creative communities is important to her. She co-founded and co-hosts the literary livestream FUMFA Poets & Writers Live (@fumfalive) with her MFA colleague and friend, fiction writer Chris Belden. She is also very interested in combining poetry with music and other creative arts. Her endeavors in this regard can be followed at @the_story_of_how. Her first chapbook, *I Used to Remember the Story of How*, was published by Finishing Line Press in 2019. Her publication credits for individual poems include *Ruminate*, *Blue Line*, *The Poetry Porch*, *The Paddock Review*, and *Collateral*. Her poem "Breath" was also nominated for a Pushcart Prize.

Vivian Shipley

Vivian Shipley's 13th book of poetry, *Hindsight:2020* (Louisiana Literature Press, SLU, 2022), was awarded the Paterson Poetry Prize for Literary Excellence. Her next collection, *On the Edge of Darkness* is forthcoming in 2024 from Louisiana Literature Press at SLU. Previous books have won NEPC's Sheila Motton Award, Word Press Poetry Prize, CT Center for the Book Poetry Prize, Paterson Poetry Prize, and CT Press Club Award for Poetry. She has also been awarded PSA's Lucille Medwick Prize, Robert Frost Foundation Poetry Prize, William Faulkner Poetry Prize and Ann Stanford Poetry Prize from USC. Shipley is the CT State University Distinguished Professor.

Joan Seliger Sidney

Joan Seliger Sidney is the Writer-in-Residence at the University of Connecticut's Center for Judaic Studies and Contemporary Jewish Life. Her published books are *Body of Diminishing Motion: Poems and a Memoir* (an Eric Hoffer Legacy Finalist, CavanKerry), *Bereft and Blessed* (AntrimHouse), and *The Way the Past Comes Back* (The Kutenai Press). Her poems and essays were published in literary journals and anthologies, including *Fast Funny Women* and *Fast Fierce Women*, also *Fast Fallen Women*, forthcoming in Woodhall Press. In addition, Sidney had several essays and poems published in recent Pure Slush anthologies, an essay published in *Gathering*, and poems published in *The Maine Review*, *HERE*, and *The Willimantic Chronicle*. *Soul House*, Sidney's translation of Mireille Gansel's *Maison d'Ame*, will be published by World Poetry Books, November 2023.

Mikayla Silkman

Mikayla Silkman is a 23-year-old writer from southwestern Connecticut. She graduated from Western Connecticut State University with a degree in Professional Writing and is studying for her MFA in Professional & Creative Writing at Western Connecticut State University. She is a devout Roman Catholic, a fan of rock music, and enjoys reading and writing fantasy and horror in addition to her poetry. She currently resides in Connecticut with her father and their two cats. In her free time, she enjoys hiking, playing video games, and spending time with her family.